The
Last
Book
You'll
Ever
Read

THE
LAST
BOOK

YOU'LL EVER READ

and other lessons from the future

FRANK OGDEN

MACFARLANE WALTER & ROSS
TORONTO

Macfarlane Walter & Ross
37A Hazelton Avenue
Toronto, Canada M5R 2E3

CANADIAN CATALOGUING IN PUBLICATION DATA

Ogden, Frank, 1920–
    The last book you'll ever read
ISBN 0-921912-56-0
1. Forecasting. 2. Twenty-first century – Forecasts. 3. Technological forecasting. I. Title.
CB161.O44 1993   303.49   C93-095004-6

Printed in the United States

This book is dedicated to those librarians, from the days of Alexandria to those in today's cloistered havens of leather and paper, who, by collecting, cataloguing, storing, and distributing the printed word in the Gutenberg format, have aided so effectively man's progress to a better understanding of our past and acceptance of our future potential.

Special thanks to my partner, companion, wife and editing disciplinarian Carol Baker for directing me along the path of (her) reality; to Anne Norman and Yvonne Van Ruskenveld of West Coast Editorial Associates for their work; and to Jim Semenick, creative hacker and fellow ten-year traveller in cyberspace, for his ability to provide the seemingly electronically impossible when required.

Contents

3 → Future Business

4 → The Everyday World

5 → *Medicine and Biotechnology*

6 → *Food and Farming*

7 → Communications

8 → Japan

9 → Education

10 → What Else Is New?

Introduction

First there were rough stick pictures sketched on the walls of caves in Lascaux, France, and Altamira, Spain. Egyptian hieroglyphics appeared on papyrus, a paperlike writing material developed about 3500 B.C. Later came the alphabet from far-off Arabia to be studied and mastered by scribes in lonely secluded monasteries. A steady job in Europe in those days was copying the Bible for a small but elite clientele – not a simple task when every word had to be written laboriously by hand.

Initially only the the illuminati of the church and then a few members of royalty were able to see a book and learn to interpret the symbols (letters and numbers). They then had to learn what the symbols meant when put into words and sentences (reading), next how to duplicate the messages (copying), and then how to create a message (writing). This literacy didn't spread, even among royalty, overnight.

A German printer, Johann Gutenberg, was the first European to develop movable type, and the first printed copy of a book – the

Bible – was printed in 1455. Fifty years before Gutenberg's type, movable type from metal molds was being used in Korea. These developments at opposite ends of the earth allowed people to record history, knowledge, and wisdom for the benefit of the following generations.

Today Gutenberg-style publications – printed books – are doomed. The vehicle that carries the words is no longer an economically viable form of transportation. Most people acquire books for the content – the words of an author or the pictures captured by a photographer on film prior to being transferred by an elaborate and costly process to paper. But the cost of the content is usually a relatively minor portion of the cost in preparing a book for the marketplace. The major cost is in building the vehicle to carry the words and images. During the five hundred years of use of Gutenberg's brilliant invention, the cost of the delivery vehicle has progressively increased to far exceed the cost of the content. Words and images are being delivered in a Lamborghini when all that is needed is a toy wagon.

The price of paper rises every year. As environmental concerns become more critical and fewer trees are harvested, prices for the cellulose to make paper are increasing dramatically. Skilled labor is shrinking. The cost of binding books can go nowhere but up. Hardcover books especially are becoming more costly to produce. Still, books are ground out in increasing numbers with less profit to all concerned, year after year. To realists, the situation is clear. The cost of producing books, even without including the cost of the content, is a nightmare for publishers.

Contrast this picture with electronic publishing on computer floppy disks or CD-ROMs (Compact Disk – Read Only Memory). Disks cost less than fifty cents each wholesale, depending on disk size, type, and manufacturer. Packaging, distribution, and marketing costs are much lower than they are for books. Computer bulletin boards lift data from one another and spread the word globally along the network. Book reviews are written at a thousand desks and sent throughout the universe to precisely the purchasers wanting such information. A new group of people has risen who can manipulate digital information profitably. These digerati communicate at the speed of light and bypass old traditional, physical highways of the past.

This low-cost network brings millions of buyers to sellers all over the planet. In its own way electronic publishing is a replay of what occurred when print first hit the masses with what were then low-cost books. Millions found a reason to learn to read and write. Publishers and ad agencies that grew with that new market will find the old game not as profitable as it once was. They will find, perhaps too late, it's not the rules that have changed but the game itself. Many in that industry will start worrying too as others, raised with the new game, become more proficient players.

All books can be sent to the purchaser electronically, delivered on any size of disk, for any type of computer; or a thousand books of 300 pages each can now be put on a single CD-ROM. This disk itself dials an 800 number that sends you the previously encoded description code (upon receipt of a valid credit card number), which automatically opens the selected volume or volumes purchased. An excellent example is the monthly photonic magazine *Nautilus*, published in Dublin, Ohio, that issues a monthly edition – a "book" in itself – plus up to 999 other books on the same disk. No printing, no binding, minimal marketing, and no costly distribution system. No minimum print run. If one copy is sold, one is released. If a million are sold, an appropriate button is pushed and a million copies are deciphered and released.

Today knowledge navigators are finding innovative ways to transfer information at dramatically lower prices. That's why this could be the last book you'll ever read.

1

The Process of Change

→ *The Importance
of Attitude*

About 150 years ago the colonization of North America began in
earnest. During the next ten decades a wave of immigration, its scope
unknown in human history, swept across America. In the main the
immigrants were ordinary people, generally unskilled, having little
formal education, and basically unprepared for the arduous life they
had chosen in the New World, a world that had none of the few
comforts of European town life.

The new settlers had one tremendous advantage. They had the
right attitude. They were open to change, wanted a new life, and
generally relished adventure. With that outlook, people learned new
skills and achieved extraordinary accomplishments. To some degree
that still happens with recent immigrants.

As we prepare to enter the third millennium, another monumental
task faces us. We must cast off the teachings of the past, just as our

forebears cast off, perhaps more willingly, what they had been taught in their homeland. We too, perhaps unknowingly, are about to migrate into another world. It will be even less familiar than the strange land viewed by the pilgrims when they landed at Plymouth Rock.

New information is being filtered and refined into new knowledge at the rate of 100 percent every eighteen months. Virtually everything we now know will be obsolete in a year and a half. With a clean slate, it is easier to learn the new. In fact, it is far easier to learn the new than be taught the past.

When I joined the Royal Canadian Air Force in 1940, wartime demands on aircraft mechanics and flight engineers were overwhelming. First of all, the few instructors available were still learning about the new airplanes and engines they had been introduced to only a few weeks previously. We all learned together. There is nothing to teach when all is new. Everyone is forced to become a learner. Within months thousands of young airmen were able to take apart and put back together a sophisticated airplane they hadn't even known about ninety days earlier. We had the right attitude. Learning was an adventure. Amazingly, the planes continued to fly and function, with very few embarrassing incidents. What we learned in months was later stretched to a lengthy course with a high-flying title that is methodically taught and goes on for years.

As we enter the third millennium, we will encounter the unfamiliar landscapes of virtual reality. We will learn, not be taught, how to create anything our imagination dictates and how to direct voice and sound to near and distant locations through what might be termed electronic ventriloquism. Biotechnology will allow (this has already started) the creation of living chimera, organisms that combine parts from two, several, or many organisms in one living creature. These combinations will not stop at bacteria, plants, or animals.

Startling developments, inventions, and innovations in fields never previously contemplated will change the way we think, work, play, and love – much like the forests, fields, mountains and streams of the New World changed the thinking, working, and playing of those immigrants from urban Europe.

The process is much the same. Only the attitude is different. We either change to meet the demands of new times or we vanish to be replaced by others more open to adventure. As this bulldozer of change rolls over our planet we have a choice: to become part of the bulldozer or part of the road.

→   *Risk in Chaos*

History is replete with stories of the alchemists of yesterday, explorers of the chemical and plant world who tried to mix, merge, and blend the many new minerals, plants, and elements just being discovered. Their main claims to fame were their attempts to create gold out of lead. That never worked, but with today's technology many things believed impossible a few years ago, never mind during the Middle Ages, are now considered probable.

In a time of chaos, the breakup of any old order brings forth the new and realigns cultures, technologies, learning, and politics. This gives rise to greater promise – the promise of a new alchemy. Not turning lead into gold (even that is remotely feasible via molecular transfer, though not yet profitable), but rather an exciting alchemy that mixes and changes culture, technology, learning, and politics, possibly forming new modes of thinking, living, learning, and working together.

Every piece of newly developed technology disturbs some firmly entrenched process. That in turn disrupts some social system, fixture, or institution. After technological disruption, nothing can return to its previous dominance. A new technology may quickly merge with another piece of only slightly older technology. A synergistic effect makes the two technologies stronger and more dynamic than either innovation operating alone. Larger social disruptions occur. A new

3

technology may be developed to bring back stability, but often it does just the opposite.

The wooden plow displaced the stick. The musket shot aside the bow and arrow. The cavalry replaced many an infantry. The car and tank, the horse. The train, the carriage. The airplane, the ship and train. Movable type replaced the scribe; the newspaper, the town crier. Television has eclipsed radio, and news is now reported as it happens, not when it is over.

Soon we will see television's merger with the computer screen. Gutenberg print is being transferred to CD-ROMs read by beams of light. Movies, long the ruler of epic scenes, are giving way to virtual reality and a cyberspace larger and more indelible than imagination itself.

It has been said that when children born today reach their eightieth birthday, 97 percent of all knowledge will have been produced *during their lifetime*. Compare this to the sixteenth century: the greatest total of knowledge then – all one could acquire in a lifetime – was about what is now contained in one *weekday* issue of the *New York Times*. Today anyone who has access to a computer, a phone line, and a modem has access, in one evening, to more information than both his or her parents had in an entire lifetime. A new learner fortunate enough to have a satellite dish can access more information in one evening than all his or her forebears in history.

There is plenty of brain capacity that we have not yet learned to use. The time may be now. These changes cannot happen over a prolonged period without producing a new species. These are evolutionary as well as revolutionary times.

In times of little change, as during the Agricultural Age, "playing it safe" was sound strategy. Even during the early days of the Industrial Age, conservatism paid off. However, as that age progressed, the risk-taker started to move up in prominence because newer fields of endeavor gave greater rewards than conventional work. The risk-takers of the early twentieth century became the barons of oil, rail, lumber, mining, fishing, retailing, and finance. Today those industries are declining as new thrones of power develop in such fields as computing, communications, biotechnology, nanotechnology, optical storage, virtual reality, and the hospitality industry.

So what to do? Prepare for what will appear to be chaos. And remember that the picture really is brighter than it looks through Industrial Age eyes. For chaos is a time of great creativity and opportunity. As the bricks of the past become unstuck and crumble there is the chance to rebuild in new and better ways.

Before the move from the Agricultural Age to the Industrial Age, people almost everywhere depended primarily on farming to earn a living. Even in North America that was 98 percent of the population. Yet during the past century most countries managed to move into the industrial era without fatal encounters. When the transition was completed, the wealth of the world had increased thirty times. Now even the poorest people live longer, starve less, enjoy more.

It will happen again, although this time the transition won't be as gradual. Much of the turbulence of river rapids is caused by the speed of change as water flows from a more tranquil river section to a narrower channel – not unlike the experience of moving from one era into another. The ride can be threatening or exhilarating, depending on your view of change.

You can view the future through the negative lens of fear or through the positive lens of opportunity. It is my belief that when the turbulence of transition finally settles down in the Communications Age, the wealth of the planet will have increased another hundred times. There are now five billion people. Many are increasing their income levels dramatically. We can all do much more now with less. Success is just an idea away.

→   *The Change*
      Quotient

For decades we have heard about IQ, the intelligence quotient that supposedly measures intelligence. Now there is a new kid on the

5

block, the CQ, or change quotient, which measures the ability to adapt to change in a changing world. As we approach the third millennium, the CQ is probably a more useful indicator of aptitude.

It is no secret that our institutions did not and do not advocate adapting to change. To do so would be contrary to definition: an institution is "an established law, custom, practice, or system; an organization having a social, educational, or religious purpose." To advocate change in institutions would have been, and still is, heresy ("any opinion opposed to official or established views"). Such thoughts are radical, also by definition: "favoring fundamental or extreme change." Over the centuries the conservative outlook has generally served a useful purpose. However, when radical change hits a culture, such change destroys the culture or society.

As the world globalizes – itself a radical change – old institutions have no sense of which direction to follow, what strategy to use, or even where to appeal for guidance. The guides are lost, and the guided are disillusioned, angry, bitter, and afraid. Where are the calm and confident in a storm of chaos? Certainly not among the leaders of the status quo, in the institutions or societies that continually advocated homage to the establishment. Outside their own boundaries, they are strangers in a strange land entering new and frightening forests.

It is worth listening to today's new knowledge navigators, often young computer hackers who seize the new technology of the day and ride it into the unknown. Theirs is a vision of hope, accomplishment, inner satisfaction, and success, not a vision of despair, terror, indecision, and poverty. They search for the unknown because they are bored with the known, and they dream of the new adventures and riches that fall to the risk-takers early in any new age.

What does this have to do with CQ, the change quotient? The new navigators, whether for genetic reasons or simply from self-motivation, have high ratings on the as-yet undrawn CQ chart. They are going where no one has gone before. Aboard caravels of silicon and gallium arsenide, today's Magellans and da Gamas are actually sailing into the unknown, although they may be the first to admit they haven't yet confirmed in which direction they are traveling. Half a millennium ago, the same could have been said of Columbus.

→   *The Next Century*

I might properly have called this section "The Ten Most Responsible and Visionary Developments of the Next Century." Or maybe the term *visionary* should precede *responsible*. Why? Because the vision must come before the thought of responsibility. An idea, a concept, or a dream may turn out to be a blessing or a curse. Hence, whether something is "responsible" is more in the eyes of the subsequent beholder than in the mind of the creator. Here are some of the most likely visionary and responsible developments for the twenty-first century.

Life Extension
When we were cave people, the dangers of the hard life limited human longevity to twenty years or less. By Roman times the average life span had advanced only to about twenty-two years. During the Dark Ages in Europe, reaching age forty was a considerable accomplishment – anywhere in the world. Even by the year 1900 if one reached the ripe old age of forty-seven years, that was considered a full life in most advanced countries. Today the average life span is about seventy-six in most westernized countries and eighty in Japan and Hong Kong.

Medical advances, especially in the marriage of biology with hard technology, will continue to accelerate. My own example comes from my weak eyesight. Glasses at age twelve thickened to "Coke bottles" by age sixty-five, and I had cataracts forming. Eye charts indicated I was into white cane country. Today, with surgically implanted lenses, my vision is 20/20 and both my driver's and helicopter/land/sea aircraft pilot's licenses have been reissued. If you think renewed vision doesn't generally extend life, you haven't been blind lately.

Such implants will become more common and will continuously improve in quality and scope during the first century of the third millennium. Today, more than six dozen body parts can be implanted in a human. If my eye implant can make me not only see better but think differently, what do you think will happen when a human becomes over 50 percent bionic?

With increasingly healthy and active lives, older people will not die before being able to leave their accumulated wisdom. With increased population and longer lives, more human imaginations will be available to help solve previously insurmountable problems.

Genetic Conception

Before the middle of the twenty-first century, children will be born outside the womb. These children, produced under conditions of genetically precise conception, will have the advantage of all the new medical and scientific knowledge that we are just now learning to understand. Outdated ideas and the fears of a "master race" will vanish, mainly because people will fear being left behind if they can't match what others are capable of accomplishing.

Young, self-trained biohackers will make startling new breakthroughs in creating new life-forms – with a basement, $50, and a "gene-blaster." They will resemble the computer hackers of the late twentieth century, without the constraints of thinking that held back the universal use of computers – until two kids, $500, and a garage showed the world how to produce a computer that created the Apple computer empire.

Government without Governments

Governments can no longer provide the basic activities governments were set up to perform. Can any government in the world protect its citizens, at home or abroad, from terrorists? Can it protect the jobs of its citizens, now that labor can be "imported" electronically?

Control fluctuations in currency? Defend borders against illegal or unwanted immigrants? Prevent an influx of environmental and cultural degradation?

Old ways don't work well anymore. Big governments can't compete, because they move so slowly. While communications move at the speed of light, governments operate like elephants with arthritis. They can no longer control information. Almost anyone, once he or she learns the ropes, can collect, interpret, and act upon critical information faster than governments. Something else, yet unknown, will replace them. When we were nomads, we had a tribal chief, then shahs and kings, and now presidents and prime ministers. Tomorrow?

Seemingly endless mountains of information, accessible to all, will bring about an end to secrecy. Present styles of governments, once the solution, have become the problem. A major improvement will evolve. We have seen the Soviet Union break up, but so will China, India, Canada, the United States, Britain, and Brazil. Many will not like the tumultuous change, but none will be able to halt it.

The Electronic Hearth

Education was once relayed from elders to younger family members. As the industrial world developed and sons went out to work, education was ordained as compulsory and turned over to a select elite carrying credentials.

During the last century "credentialism" became a form of knowledge licensing – following a restricted path dictated by those already holding the necessary documents, who fitted others into the assembly line. It's an assembly line not only of factories but also of people and a linear world of *ABCs* and 123s, mapped out by academic planners promising continuous employment, a house in the suburbs, and a reward of retirement with generous government and company pensions. In the relatively slow-moving Industrial Age, this worked. Times are changing. Cracks are apparent. Education, modified by modern electronics and photonics, is returning to the home.

As communication modes, speeds, translations, and graphics grow and change, knowledge of the world will become more readily available to all. Satellite dishes now bring me 200 video channels, one thousand radio channels, electronic newspapers, magazines, and an encyclopedia. This information is available to all people who have learned how to tap these new fountains of beneficial knowledge. No public education institution can match this knowledge because the same arthritis that crippled governments has spread to most other Industrial Age institutions, including schools.

The Brain

Humans have learned more about the human brain during the past decade than ever before. "Information overload" is a myth. We are probably using only 1 percent of our brain power and it's time we learned to use the other 99 percent. The Computed Axial Tomography (CAT) scan has shown us the cranium. Magnetic Resonance Imaging (MRI) has shown us the gray and white matter. The Positron Emission Tomography (PET) scanner has shown us where we think (a different part of the brain lights up when we think work rather than play).

Now Quantified Signal Imaging (QSI) is showing *what* we think! What we learn in this field will change everyday life more than the automobile did. During the early years of the twenty-first century, people will be inputting on computers and editing video with thought waves; they'll be creating artistic masterpieces without physically touching canvas, clay, or a musical instrument. This new creativity will change the world more than Gutenberg's print.

Safe and Sufficient Water

In the field of global health, the biggest bang for the buck comes from providing clean water to humankind. As environmental consciousness continues to increase, people will establish new priorities, and water purity will become even more important, especially when the world realizes that cleaning existing water is cheaper and easier than finding new supplies. Immense filtration plants using innovative techniques and processes will sprout up. According to 1987 figures, developed countries average a gross national product of around $11,300. Developing countries average only $640. With about 75 percent of the world's population living in countries with a low income, pure water there equates with survival. One-quarter of the world's population – 1.2 billion residents of those countries – do not have access to safe drinking water. It is estimated that 250 million people in Africa, about 40 percent of that continent's population, will suffer or die as a result of water-related troubles in the next decade. In developing countries about 25 million are dying now from unsafe water; 60 percent are children. One thousand children die every hour from diarrhea. Clean water will dramatically reduce this disgrace.

Global Power Grid

Almost fifty years ago, the American genius Buckminster Fuller proposed that the electrical power grid of the United States be linked to its U.S.S.R. counterpart. Unfortunately, post–World War II political considerations on both sides put that possibility aside. The concept is surprisingly simple. Hook up the American electrical power network, through the Canadian power network, over the north polar region to the Russian network anywhere between Vladivostok and Murmansk.

Why? When it is daylight and the United States is power-hungry, power could flow to North America. When it is night here, power could flow into the Russian network. A win-win situation. Water now wastefully flowing over dams during the night in either country would be harnessed to be beneficial elsewhere. It would save fortunes that are spent on standby coal and oil peak-period generating plants. As with many problems, the solution involves not so much technology as it does arranging the necessary sociological and conceptual channels.

Food Diversity

Purveyors of doom claim that plant and animal diversity is decreasing at a rapid rate. Yet in just the past few years, life-forms that never existed before, with previously unheard of abilities, have been created. The antifreeze gene from the winter flounder now resides in the Atlantic salmon, allowing it too to swim in below-freezing waters. That same antifreeze gene from fish has also been inserted into the canola plant, making it freeze-resistant to early frosts.

The gene that causes the "glow" in a firefly has been transferred across the "impenetrable" barrier from animal to plant! This is the new diversity. Its growth will blossom. DNA revitalization will resurrect lost species.

Virtual Reality

Until recently we only experienced – physically, intellectually, and emotionally – what we actually experienced. Artificial, or virtual, reality is about to change the way we experience, the way we view "reality," the way we learn, and the way we think. Although the common term is now virtual reality, *artificial* better explains these other forms of reality, because the word *virtual* carries an "almost there" quality about it. Artificial reality can take us up to "there" and then beyond any reality previously known.

The simplest example of functioning virtual reality is the Powerglove, manufactured for use with Nintendo games. The Powerglove is a long, sleeve-type glove that contains, in essence, a computer terminal. When an appropriate button is pressed, the glove knows where it is in relation to your television set. It can then control the action on the screen. Now an advanced type of glove allows supermarket shopping without leaving your chair. You turn on your TV set, see the grocery store interior, put on your glove, and as you "stroll" through the aisles (still sitting in your armchair at home), reach out with the glove, which will electronically penetrate your TV screen, and pick up, for example, a bottle of Heinz ketchup. Description and price are indicated in an upper corner of your screen. You "drop" the purchase into your electronic cart and proceed to the next purchase. No waiting at the checkout counter. Your tally is your checkout. Tied in with forthcoming refrigerated "mailboxes," purchases will be delivered (in actuality) to your driveway fridge, whether you are home or not. Insert a credit card and your driveway fridge opens up to reveal unmelted ice cream and crisp lettuce.

In other fields, the Powerglove would allow a robot or an android to operate on someone on a space station by following the movements of a surgeon on earth operating on a robot patient. The same telemetry that tells us about astronauts in space will work in the other direction and tell the operating robot what moves to make.

Possibilities for this amazing new field go much further. By wearing a sensor outfit similar to a wetsuit, you will be able to have experiences such as wrestling a grizzly bear (if that's your thing) with no physical danger. Once in the experience, though, you might forget that it is an artificial reality and really believe that it's happening to you. Excitement levels will be very high. This may do more to reduce drug abuse than anything else to date because you will be able to get experiences via electronics/photonics that are perhaps superior to trips from hallucinatory drugs. What better way to learn about life in the Arctic than to drive your own dog team across the tundra? With virtual reality, you could live out any fantasy, alone or with a companion. Safe sex is almost here! Such experiences, or something similar, are already possible on prototype units in experimental stages at various research centers around the world.

The Liberation of Technology

Changes in technology will alter the way we live, the way we love, the way we think, the way we dream, the way we create. We are moving from a lowly state as worker caterpillars into creative bionic butterflies. Working our way out of the chrysalis is like escaping from a dark crypt. After a momentous struggle, what emerges is not what existed before. With such massive changes, old ways of thinking and of handling change will also change, because they too do not work.

The butterfly doesn't operate like a caterpillar and is not grounded by gravity. Like the emerging butterfly, we have left our formative stage.

→ *Future Survival*
Guide

1. If you are not there already, start preparing to switch to a sunrise field from a sunset field. (A sunrise field is a new industry at the beginning of a learning and profit curve; young, vibrant, and innovative methods are used to create a product or service in demand; it has no way to go but up. A sunset field is an industry near the end of its life span with products or services that are in decreasing demand and have usually been superseded by new technologies.) Remain alert for change. Word processing is still relatively new, but it will soon be obsolete as voice-activated terminals replace the present keyboards and word-processing secretaries.

2. Don't specialize. Train for a flexible attitude and an open state of mind. Question everything you have ever learned. Did you receive an education or an indoctrination? Your culture can be your prison.

3. Minimize investment in fixed nonportable assets. Rent; don't buy. Everything that's really important today is still invisible because we haven't yet started to produce the viewing "window" for the Information Age.

4. Embrace and learn to understand the new technologies. You can't get in on the ground floor after a new industry is already established. Don't even wait for the ground floor. Look for the excavations!

5. Knowledge is doubling every eighteen months (most of it now coming from outside North America). It is impossible to know everything about anything. Your best hope is to learn how to access information. Utilize new, nontraditional methods for your continuing education. This can be via satellite, fiber-optics, videocassette, interactive video disks, and computer-driven information systems and data bases. Your biggest mistake may be your unwillingness to pay for information.

6. Assume more personal individual responsibility.

7. Do not rely on big government, big business, or big unions. Indoctrination and training from the Industrial Age is no longer an asset; in the new world it is a definite liability. In a rapidly changing environment, the specialist can become obsolete overnight.

8. Reduce nonessential expenditures. Always live below your means so that a drop in your income will not create a crisis. In addition, your fiscal strategy should plan for continuous upgrading of new technology.

9. Prepare to be highly mobile. Don't get locked into Industrial Age virtues like nationalism and patriotism. In the Communications Age the action goes to the mobile. Environments conducive to economic flowering will change rapidly as cities, states, and countries vie for ideas and information.

10. Be self-employed or you may be unemployed.

2

The Work Force in Transition

→ *Where Have
the Jobs Gone?*

Not so many years ago, no passenger elevator moved without an operator. Utility services needed sweating men to dig ditches for phone, water, and sewer lines. And what about gas station attendants, streetcar conductors, typewriter repairers, stenographers, train firemen, printbox typesetters, linotype operators, and hydro meter readers? Most are going, or have gone, to that big unemployment center in the sky.

What has replaced them? Computers, automated teller machines, fax machines, and other machines. Even machines are being replaced – by machines that do multiple jobs, such as the E-mail modem/fax/answering machine that does three jobs in one, at half the price of last year's single-unit fax machine. If your job can be replaced by a machine, even one not yet invented, start retraining now. Global competition dictates it. If your company cannot match the productivity of overseas robots on the dull, monotonous, repetitive jobs that still exist, be assured some foreign operation has already got that market targeted.

If your work is tied to what used to be called a "natural resource," don't expect to be working at your present job until you retire. Your job or even the industry itself won't be around. While Viceroy of India, Lord Mountbatten presided over the end of the British Empire. Today union leaders in the forest industry are in a similar position – the army of lumberjacks is shrinking rapidly. Even the word is now outdated. No amount of promotional "creativity" can make these jobs come back again.

Plastic is replacing steel. Ceramics, vinyl, and new materials are replacing wood, steel, and other building materials. Molecular engineers are developing materials that never existed before, materials that will be "assembled" molecule by molecule, with a strength that will make steel look weak. New materials can now be created, much like nylon replacing silk in stockings, from atmospheric materials at a much lower cost than the natural way of the past.

Postal delivery, which once dominated the day's office work, is fast being replaced by E-mail, faxes, and telephones. The answering machine is replacing the receptionist, the automated bank machine is replacing human bank tellers, and voice navigators are replacing secretaries. No job is sacred. Even the Vatican now broadcasts messages via satellite. It is hard to believe, but jobs are following the same path as slavery, child labor, and indentured service as a way of using human energy to provide a service, enhance a culture, or provide an income for the population.

For years now the official (and memorable) logo of the Japanese Industrial Robot Society has been an image of a stainless-steel-gloved robot hand releasing humans from their position as a lowly caterpillar into a creative and beautiful butterfly. That indelible image may mean more than initially intended.

Almost everybody today, with the possible exception of some government and union leaders, is aware that our old skills cannot command the respect and pay levels they did in the past. They just are not salable anymore. No matter what training we take, our skills will only be viable for a short period and then we will have to retrain for something else, quite likely something radically different. Although I am a futurist today, if I don't continue to change, by tomorrow I will be a historian.

Flexibility is the key to tomorrow. Constant retraining will be essential. Tomorrow will be the age of task forces, a time when groups will gather to work on projects and then disband. Such groups already work around the world on major construction projects, putting out oil fires in Kuwait, setting up Expo sites, or creating movies.

Since the fall of the Hollywood studio, new, more adaptive producers have bypassed the old way and now assemble the talent and the organization to make one movie. After it is over, whether it be a hit or a bust, everyone scatters. The next movie may or may not have some of the players that produced the last epic. The latest buzzword for this type of instant "rise and fall" organization is "virtual corporation."

The rush from the past to the future is constantly shortening the time before anything current becomes a historical artifact. The average shelf life of any consumer electronic product in Tokyo is now a mere ninety days. What used to take five years now occurs in one.

Every technological invention, along with the innovative ways in which it is used, changes the world around it – not only technologically, but also socially, economically, and personally. Many people trying to survive on unemployment insurance, workers' compensation, and welfare are on a downhill slide – into the land of the techno-peasant. Once there, they become outcasts because they are resisting tomorrow, grounded in the past. The devastating net result will be reminiscent of the turn of the century for people who did not learn to read and write.

Yet with all the unemployment in the fading industries of yesteryear, there is still action in the growth fields of tomorrow. Most of this new energy starts on a small scale. Often a few coworkers, partners, or shareholders produce remarkable sales volumes. Many small companies with a staff of only ten are knocking out $5 million worth of product a year. That's $500,000 per employee or partner. With that output, the company can afford to pay up to $100,000 a year to productive knowledge workers. And these people are developing the personal confidence to go almost anywhere on the planet and earn a comparable income. They are highly mobile, flexible beyond belief, and not bound by nationalism – they are truly planetary citizens. Every country needs them and the virtual corporations they create, and smart countries are out prospecting for them.

You may think it is impossible to have a company where the average employee can produce $500,000 a year. Well, it's almost being done today at Apple Computers. Revenue per employee is $437,100. That's twice what IBM is accomplishing and four times what competitor Digital Equipment Corp. has been able to produce. If Toyota can handle the planet with fewer than a hundred thousand workers, why does General Motors need more than that to handle just the United States?

Look at the government financial aid supplied every year to developing countries (or to Indian reservations). It is like providing fish instead of fishhooks, and enslaves the recipient in servitude forever – or until the rules are changed. More sophisticated givers provide the fishhooks, encouraging independence and a continuing supply of fish.

Once you learn how to swim, the acquired skills work in rivers, lakes, pools, quarries, and oceans. Those who can't swim quickly encounter aquatic hazards. The same applies to salable personal skills for tomorrow. The difference between the "knows" and the "know-nots" is not a matter of race, color, formal education, or even economics. It is attitude. Information can lead to knowledge. Knowledge can lead to wisdom. And wisdom can lead to power. Information is easier to access now than at any time in human history. But without the right attitude and the energy to go out and explore, present-day prospectors will be like those who sat at home and missed the adventure, the danger, and the glory of the Gold Rush.

→   *Retraining*

In 1978 Digital Equipment of Maryland built the VAX 780 mini-computer. It was about three feet high, three feet wide, and six feet long, and it cost $30,000 to manufacture. Six years later the same company came out with a microchip the size of a fingernail that cost $300 and replaced the VAX 780. The highly skilled, highly paid workers who produced and serviced the VAX 780 were no longer required. They were obliged to retrain. Since they were in the vanguard of the computer business, retraining in the computer industry wasn't too stressful. But for someone coming into computers cold and having worked perhaps only three months on a VAX 780, it was stressful to have to move to another segment of the industry.

When airlines flew internal combustion engines with propellers, the engine mechanics worked about one hour for every hour of flight time per engine. In the dying days of the prop business, the early 1960s, most airlines were flying four-engine aircraft. So every four-engine airplane that flew eight hours required thirty-two hours of maintenance. Four skilled mechanics each put in eight hours on an engine to keep the aircraft fit to fly the next flight.

Then one day the jet engine appeared. It flew and flew and flew, and its engines required little maintenance. Because it was almost never "down," it kept flying – sometimes up to twenty hours a day. Maintenance costs dropped, and many highly skilled engine mechanics had to retrain. The same thing has occurred now that fuel injection has replaced carburetors in automobile engines. With fuel injection, it is easy to change the computer card that regulates fuel injection and send the defective unit back to the factory, where a robot reconditions it. A skilled mechanic is not required to do that.

Today change comes with the whirling wind. In a swift-moving small company, one staff member might have ten jobs in five years. These are not just variations of a job but distinctively different jobs, because traditional jobs have been vanishing as computers and software have replaced manual bookkeeping, dictation, filing, and operating Gestetner machines and typewriters. Even the switchboard operator once employed by every fair-sized firm is gone.

Telex machines usually had operators who processed everyone's messages, as they had earlier processed cables and telegrams before handing them over to others trained to dispatch them around the world. Now people not only send their own faxes and E-mail, they also compose what they send – without a secretary. Middle management executives, unfamiliar with many of the new techniques, find out one day that retraining is necessary – their old jobs have disappeared too.

And this is just the beginning. Every technological change changes some type of job somewhere. It also causes sociological change. The switch from postal service to courier and fax has been reducing daily trips to the post office, facilitating more rapid communication, and putting stress on postal workers. They must retrain.

Since newly required skills are scarce, workers trained for the future command top money, better working conditions, and various fringe benefits. Some companies, such as those in computer software, may have to cater to the type of worker that is now in demand. Otherwise business falters. This is the other side of the unemployment picture. Business owners have to change too and perhaps relocate to somewhere that might not be their first choice. That move might be across town, to a faraway city or, more likely, across the world.

Something else is happening amid this rapid change in the workplace. Since anyone trained for the past possesses outdated learning, of little value in the global marketplace, the basic requirement when hiring a new employee is attitude. Potential employees (from janitor to president) with the right attitude can rapidly absorb new training. If they have the wrong attitude, hiring them just brings endless headaches. In my seminars around the world I tell companies: "Hire on attitude alone. Credentials are from the past, and past skills are obsolete, as we all witness every day." For example, in the new field of virtual reality there are, as yet, no experts, except the few inventors, innovators, and developers working on the early prototypes, just now emerging. This field will be as big as oil, steel, and aviation have been in the past. This new Orville has just made the first flight – and no one else in the world knows how to do it! Imagine the opportunities.

The only constant is change. Learn to love it. As the rate of change accelerates, the result will appear chaotic to the uninitiated. But there is elegant order in chaos. Few so far have learned to recognize it and profit from it. This is where the future lies.

→   ## A New
Caste System?

In the 1880s indentured laborers were imported into North America to build the transcontinental railroads and to provide labor for the forest industry. Immigrants from such countries as India and China got their first view of North America via the west coast ports of North America.

It took many lumberjacks to produce what today would be considered a small output. By the 1950s a typical west coast sawmill employed up to a thousand people, considerably fewer than in earlier times. A modern mill, cutting perhaps twice the volume of an earlier twentieth-century operation, may employ only a hundred people. The reduction in work force resulted from the rather rustic "automation" introduced between the two world wars. World War II provided the era of high-speed, high-volume production.

With the high cost of raw materials today, companies are forced to focus on value instead of volume. What steps are required to make this possible? Sounds like going into reverse, but the solution in this case is to add more labor. Since our Northern American labor rates are among the highest in the wood world, how is it viable when several factors make Americans and Canadians poor candidates for globalization?

Answer: set up a two-tiered labor structure. The original highly skilled operators of the automation equipment do what they do best and stay at the high (perhaps $30) hourly rate; the added-value activity takes place in another company's plant that handles subcontracting (at around $10 an hour). Higher value-added, higher productivity, but at less cost. It keeps the companies viable, but it also brings back indentured labor.

What are the social consequences of such a twin-level society? What is the next step? Will such operations follow the Japanese model where the main contractor, say Toyota, pays a high wage-and-benefit package to core employees, but outsources jobs requiring lower skills to subcontractors who pay their workers a considerably lower rate?

This has great potential for people in higher wage brackets. The new system allows the company to once more become economically viable, but on the backs of the lower-paid, less-educated, unskilled employees. Fewer union members with more protected benefits have stability and a secure future, but the smaller numbers reduce union strength.

It was once believed that a high-speed, high-volume process was the answer. Now it appears that smaller volume with higher value-added input is the road to the future. It's interesting to ponder the implications for towns with such an obvious chasm between different sets of workers established next door to one another. Could this be the caste system of tomorrow?

→ ## The Old
   Caste System

North Americans pride themselves on their version of democracy. "Everybody is equal" is the political cry. That simply isn't true.

Indeed, our caste system may be the cause of our decline in the new world order. Consider how we view people by job classification. The factory sweeper is a "common laborer" and gets paid minimum wage or close to it. People on the factory floor are "blue-collar workers," paid an hourly wage. Office workers are "white-collar" or "pink-collar" workers and receive a fixed salary. Engineers and computer programmers are viewed as "nerds." Without any of the above, the operation would quickly come to a halt, yet that vision doesn't seem to penetrate management. Management sees that work force as flexible, meaning that the number in the work force can be increased or decreased as demand requires – much like increasing or decreasing the plant's electrical power requirements. The effect on attitude is disastrous.

In North America it is more lucrative and long-lasting to move into management, finance, or marketing. Increasingly the best minds have been traveling in that direction. It wasn't always thus. During America's best times – the 1950s and 1960s – veterans from World War II, in many instances, chose engineering. A victorious nation rewarded them by plowing vast sums into educational opportunities that gave the cream of the survivors opportunities never before available. They produced innovative products and systems, not just on earth with unmatched highway systems, but also in the air and beyond. These were directly attributable to that investment in the new education of the day. It provided the intellectual thrust that propelled the Industrial Age.

In North America today there are more lawyers confronting, delaying, obstructing, litigating, and destroying what that earlier group built up than there are engineers trying to build anew. When there are more lawyers than engineers in any sizable political district you can expect more trouble than triumph. And that's what we are reaping now.

When a lawyer can pull in an annual salary of $200,000, it can't help affecting young high-school students considering a career. Imagine those classy offices, a corporate Mercedes, partnership bonuses, and unlimited expense accounts, along with what (up to now) has appeared to be a more socially acceptable pedestal. It's an environment that is ruled by the precedent of the past, that resists new intellectual thinking, and where the heaviest physical thing ever lifted is the phone or an American Express card. How does that look compared with actually getting your hands dirty while working in merely adequate quarters and being paid the "industry standard"? North America is now paying, and paying dearly, for this economic caste system.

Management raised in such a system forces engineers and designers to listen more to marketing forces than to creative ones, more to bottom-line results for the next quarter than to long-term success and survival of the company. Dumb. Especially when, with proper social incentives and availability of training, that floor sweeper can come up with another $7 billion idea equal to the one Steve Jobs and Steve Wozniak developed in their garage.

Are any North American companies seeing the world through this type of visionary eye? A few. In Prince Albert, Saskatchewan, the Weyerhaeuser Corporation plant has introduced "the fifth shift" system. One week out of five, a shift of the entire production labor force attends in-house classes to update training, not just for their present job or the next one they may be promoted to, but also the one after that. It is done in-house because no academic institution has the equipment to train workers for the new fields this company is moving into. Wait until the company's competition feels the results of that investment.

→   ## The Changing
     Work Force

In recent years there has been a trend for big-city residents to move to less densely populated areas. Today's technology, which allows many workers (especially in the communications segment) to operate from almost anywhere, is accelerating the migration. Those moving may be the elite of tomorrow.

"Community" is taking on a new connotation. We used to think of that word as meaning "people living in a particular district" or "a social unit within a larger one and having interests, work, etc., in common." Geographic proximity is no longer required. Now members of a social unit may be scattered around the globe. As electronic nomad Steven K. Roberts, head honcho at Nomadic Research Labs of California, says, "As long as your head is in cyberspace it doesn't matter where your body is." Roberts, usually "on the road" with his bike, is in touch with the world via satellite, radio, computer modem, cellular phone, and three computers. He even types as he rides. His is an example of one of the new lifestyles. He is also an example of how the centrifugal forces that once bound societies together are now tearing them apart. But he has found how to create a lifestyle both rewarding and profitable by doing what was, until recently, impossible.

Miners, who dig into the earth, and farmers, who till the soil, now make up a mere 2 percent of the U.S. work force and 3 percent of the Canadian work force, down from 98 percent two hundred years ago. Workers who still make things, conducting repetitive movements for high-volume manufacturers, compose about 10 percent of the current labor force in the United States (25 percent in Canada). Those highly skilled blue-collar workers from the Industrial Age, because of downsizing and advancing technology, have not been able to retain their previously high-paying occupations. Their future is uncertain.

Such service personnel as maids, waitresses, janitors, taxi operators, and store clerks are also performing repetitive tasks, but generally on a one-to-one basis; they now form 30 percent of the work force. Eventually, almost everyone who manufactures a product or performs a service that can be replaced by a machine will be replaced by a machine. With inflation, about a third of these people already are falling behind in their standard of living.

That still leaves almost 60 percent. The rising, and in many cases rapidly rising, segment is the top 20 percent of the work force that perform analytic or creative services for the Communications Age, services that can be sold worldwide and consist of problem solving or problem identifying or brokering of strategic activities. This field favors writers; video producers; scientists; engineers; free or abstract thinkers; people willing to risk, experiment, or collaborate; legal or banking executives; and eclectic consultants. Their skills are portable and in demand everywhere.

Those who learn to operate in a vastly changed and still-changing global environment; those who can walk on quicksand and dance with electrons; those who amass an array of varied experiences; those who see connections where others see chaos – they will flourish and find opportunity in every disturbance. These people are usually from families with parents interested in their development and progress. They closely safeguard their health, travel widely for both work and learning, read a lot, and comprehend the benefits of computer literacy. These people have nowhere to go but up.

The almost 35 percent who can't find employment in the fast-fading industrial marketplace will become a subclass of techno-peasants, politely called unemployables. This group has increased rapidly in the last few years. They may lack education or skills or be socially unacceptable because of their attitude, alcohol or drug dependence, or basic ignorance of what is happening around them. Many do not show up on unemployment rolls because they have given up or think they are too old to retrain. One recent report says that today 60 percent of North Americans are not carrying their own economic weight – they take more out of the economy than they put into it. This would mean that Japan is in control of a larger productive working population than the United States, even though the United States has twice the population of Japan. Techno-peasants will face bleak futures. They will inherit what's left of most big cities.

Current population growth projections show techno-peasants

increasing at a rate double or triple that of analytic/creative workers. One surprise: Those with degrees are 2.5 times more likely to be laid off than the average worker (this includes service workers). Ten percent will never work again.

Here's a social economic breakdown of the work force in transition:

Earth workers	2% and falling
Production workers	10% and falling
Service workers	30% and rising slowly
Analytic/creative workers	20% and rising rapidly
Techno-peasants	35% and rising rapidly
Moving between worlds	3%
Total	100%

→ *"Home"*
Companies

Two decades ago came the cry "Small is beautiful." By 1988 Statistics Canada reported that 62 percent of all new net jobs in Canada were coming from companies with five or fewer employees. A year later 82 percent of new jobs came from companies with ten or fewer employees. There is a similar but more gradual trend in the United States. At this rate, in ten years more than two-thirds of the work force will work for very small companies. With today's technology, companies require few employees to produce a high dollar-value of business.

Meanwhile, what is happening to the large companies that used to hire thousands, make large contributions to political parties, and provide the foundation of union strength? Everything now seems to be moving to empower small companies and weaken these large ones. Technology provides laser beams to small, gazelle-like companies. The big outfits, illiterate to the new times, end up able to use only bows and arrows.

Even as governments pass new legislation to "protect" failing large companies, that same legislation works toward the fracturing of the business world and the benefit of small companies that can be run from the home. When proposed legislation states that all companies with twenty or more employees must be unionized, for example, that gives rise to small companies with, say, fifteen employees, below the threshold of the new law. There are now dozens of such legislative incentives to stay small. It wasn't the way government expected the law to work, but governments aren't into reality.

Small companies can move fast – in or out of any community, province, state, or country. Electrons traveling at the speed of light make it possible. Meanwhile the old system of government, requiring ever more taxes, piles on more burdens for those that still play the old game. Large companies, old political parties, and old executives who still play the same game find empires disintegrating under their feet.

Small companies don't have to carry the union costs of unrealistically high wages, rigid working regulations, and the disruptive and financial burden of strikes. So the small company is continually in a position to steal some of the large organization's customers every time a problem arises. How many times can this occur before the large company becomes bankrupt? But more than that is happening: as more people become "clients" or "partners" they become interdependent. They become nicer to one another. Service improves. Big business can't do that.

There are other invisible effects. Money moves rapidly via electronic winds to gentler lands. Entrepreneurs so urgently required to instigate and maintain a vibrant economy depart for more attractive environs or are persuaded to move by the inducements offered by learning how the new game is played. Small *is* beautiful, and it's getting more beautiful all the time. To ignore what is happening, to think that the old ways will eventually return, is the route to economic suicide.

→   *The Fifth Sphere*

One of the barometers helpful in spotting trends is the emergence of small newsletters dealing with one topic. A new one has just hit my desk. It's called "The Fifth Sphere" and it deals with "telecommuting," the buzzword for moving work to the workers (as opposed to moving workers to their work).

The definition of the Fifth Sphere was originally conceived by the Japanese Ministry of International Trade and Industry (MITI), the government bureaucracy generally given credit for the rise of "Japan Inc." This is its vision of twenty-first-century life:

- Age of the First Sphere. Before the transition to modern society, there was but one human environment. The home and the workplace were combined in one place and formed a single sphere. The age of the First Sphere continued for a long time.

- Division into the Second Sphere. As industrialization and modernization progressed after the industrial revolution, separation of the workplace from the home accelerated, and the workplace became an independent Second Sphere; that is, home and workplace were divided.

- Emergence of the Third Sphere. As the modernization of industry and society advanced, a Third Sphere, recreation, emerged as an independent realm in addition to home and work, distinct from those two and functioning in its own right. The importance of this sphere is rising steadily in everyday life. This sphere, in some ways, typifies the modern urban environment.

- Increasing Demand for a Fourth Sphere. Developed nations that built sophisticated, industrialized societies were able to attain great convenience and comfort in life but, at the same time, suffered the drawback of centralized control. Urban residents now find it necessary to liberate themselves from psychological and physical stresses and to restore health by escaping from everyday life and immersing themselves in nature. Combined with the diversification of lifestyles and values, the need for resorts for extended stays is rapidly growing.

This new development can, however, be interpreted as only a transfer of the Third Sphere in time and location and an extension of conventional lifestyle – not really a Fourth Sphere in the true sense.

- Leap to the Fifth Sphere. The attainment of a twenty-first-century lifestyle requires an environment that is not residential or industrial in function and is not convention- and resort-oriented. It must have all the elements of the four spheres but at the same time be a city not classifiable under any one of them – in other words, it must be a Fifth Sphere, a new type of city.

After setting the above definitions, the Japanese are moving ahead with plans for such a new $50 billion city. They call it a "multifunctionopolis" and it will be located near Adelaide, Australia. This is the grandest scheme for this concept, but Chiba Prefecture in Japan already boasts an established research and development park of 250 acres with Fujitsu, the largest computer company in Japan, setting up a million-square-foot facility to accommodate ten thousand new-age workers. This and all such future developments worldwide will likely be linked.

When a concept like telecommuting starts out, growth is slow at first. Then it explodes. It is another example of an economic effect that perhaps does not slip into public consciousness for years.

As of 1993, I have been telecommuting for seventeen years. For me it is definitely the way to go. When I started, few people except artists and writers were doing the same. Now a reported 17 percent of the working population in western Canada and 10 percent in eastern Canada are telecommuting.

And it is developing in ways many people would consider strange: New York Life Insurance Company is having application and claim forms processed by telecommuters in Ireland (the company can't find enough people who can spell in New York). Large credit card companies are having client chits processed in the Caribbean. You can get income tax and accounting done in Madras, India, for a fraction of the cost here. Those who operate in this way realize their market is no longer merely local or regional, but the whole five billion people on the planet.

→ *Teleworking*

If you are already working from home or planning to do so, your future is probably bright. Recent studies indicate that "teleworking" appeals to forward thinkers, who already have higher status and visibility than in-house office workers and show higher productivity. As well, they are reported to be happier, living higher quality lives, and – in companies that have productivity bonuses – making more money. Many consultants, writers, computer programmers, financial analysts, researchers, and desktop publishers are rapidly climbing the economic totem pole.

Teleworking covers many categories of "remote" work where individuals conduct their duties away from a permanent location. As we enter the Communications Age, a substantial segment of the work force, especially in knowledge industries, will be operating from other than the traditional office location. The implications for everyone will be enormous.

About 10 percent of the work force operates from home full time, with another 10 percent operating from home part-time. This does not include executives who may bring home their "office-in-a-briefcase" every night. It seems almost assured, partly because of the drop in the cost of telecommunications, that teleworking has nowhere to go but up.

Occupations most suitable for teleworking tend to be information-intensive rather than capital-intensive. They are particularly evident, at this early stage of the Information Age, in the financial, computer, research, and publishing sectors.

Teleworking provides employers with greater access to a wider talent pool. By using scarce resources more effectively, companies improve profitability. Theoretically, teleworkers could be employed half a physical world away from where they live. This can be either frightening or attractive, depending on your confidence.

Flexibility in home and work relationships and the substantial reduction in travel time and expenses are the main advantages for the employee. It becomes questionable just how much of an employee the worker-at-home becomes, as he or she requires more self-discipline – usually associated with the self-employed. Studies indicate that teleworkers enjoy the independence and freedom of working at home and the resulting closer family relationships. Many seem to prefer or not to notice the lack of conventional social contacts that a regular nine-to-five office regime offers.

Some sales people, auditors, building inspectors, and others were conducting work-from-home operations even before the Communications Age began to blossom. Today laptop and plug-into-the-nearest-phone computers, worldwide 800 numbers, and communications networks can broaden their field of coverage. When computer communications via direct-to-satellite connections became available on Japan Air Lines in 1992, another whole field of accessibility opened. We now have foreign opportunities for accessing information and dispatching it to the home office, from sea level or from 36,000 feet in the sky.

Some fifty American companies, several belonging to the Fortune 500, have so far instigated formal telework programs. You can bet that many others will soon follow suit.

→ *The One-Person*
    Office

Statistics Canada has revealed some astounding facts. Almost 90 percent of all new jobs in Canada are being created by new companies with twenty or fewer employees. About 62 percent of the total work force works for companies with five or fewer employees, and 82 percent for companies with ten or fewer staff. It's not only computers that are getting smaller.

But how many operations have only one or two staff? They may be tomorrow's surprise. Why? Because they may be doing a greater dollar value of business and showing more net profit per person than companies only slightly larger. A surprising number of very small companies have "gone global" – a possibility never even considered in the past. They are able to do this because we have reached a level of technical competence today that allows us to perform with so few people. This is another reason why large companies have to downsize to survive. Smaller companies will steal away their business.

That this number of solo entrepreneurs could possibly increase or even raise the per-person productivity level seems incomprehensible. But with today's technology and what is already in the pipeline, it appears likely. Government action is the cause of the speeded-up process. This wasn't the way it was planned, but then governments are the last to recognize what I call The Law of Unintended Results: Any law, rule, regulation, or sanction conceived with Industrial Age thinking reverses itself in a Communications Age environment.

Governments, in a move to appease workers in failing old-style factories, try to support such companies financially, even though such companies are no longer viable. In so doing, governments pass such laws as making company officials responsible for separation pay, vacation pay, pension payments, unpaid salaries, and taxes. Governments lay down laws about who shall be unionized. They put into effect a permanent hiring freeze. Net result: they stifle jobs, instead of saving or increasing jobs. But this makes small companies very efficient.

In Germany there is the mid-size equivalent, the Mittelstrand, similar to our small companies in Canada. All these companies have fewer than five hundred employees. The Mittelstrand produce 67 percent of the German Gross National Product (GNP) and 30 percent of the exports. Their portion of German exports totals $421 billion, topping exports by mid-size companies in both the United States ($394 billion) and Japan ($286 billion). The Mittelstrand spend 20 percent annually on research and development and up to $18,000 a year to train each apprentice for four years. Apprentices are selected and hired while still in school.

What is about to happen will be a boon to one-person companies. It is something that until now was just not possible – to input direct thought into a computer. One person will soon be able to use the mind alone – along with a bit of technology – to edit videotape or printed copy.

Those who first latch onto this emerging technique will have unbelievable power, certainly more than a larger operation not aware of how to capitalize on the marriage of mind and technology. Production by such a person will exceed anything known in the past. Decision making will take microseconds and the finished project will take a fraction of the time, cost, and materials formerly required. Profits will be astronomical but the market price will be lower than what would have to be charged to produce the same product with our present system. Such effective one-person operations will have virtually no competition.

→   *After Retirement?*
         Work

Remember when you first got hit with reality? After working hard all your life, you dreamed of the day when your kids would be old enough to get a job, leave the nest, and let you retire in justified leisure. In fact, more than two million retired North Americans are now back on the job. A *U.S. News & World Report* poll shows that 45 percent of respondents either already are or expect to be working after age sixty-five. That means almost half of that population segment won't be in the leisure class as soon as they originally anticipated. One benefit: working appears to keep you healthy much longer. And many retirees quickly tire of experiencing just another day like Saturday used to be. Six months of doing nothing can be dangerous for many retirees.

In the United States this issue is climbing up the political agenda. Social Security recipients may soon be allowed to retain a much larger portion of benefits while tackling the back-to-work trail. At the moment people in the age bracket sixty-five to sixty-nine have $1 in $3 clawed back when they earn more than $10,200. (It's much, much worse in Canada.) But recent legislation will move the exemption ceiling up to $20,000 by 1997. A pending Senate law would abolish any ceiling.

The elderly aiding the elderly appears to be one of the hotter markets for back-to-workers. *World Report* says home health aides can expect a 92 percent increase in demand for services by 2005, the largest increase in any field. Retiring health-care workers won't have to miss a day between working/retirement/working again. Some retirees are setting up their own companies in the health-care supply field, finding, screening, training, and placing retirees.

Another hot spot is to fill gaps in corporations that have unexpected employment holes. They would rather hire temporary help at slightly higher wages than have more staff on a permanent payroll that is becoming harder and harder to reduce. Also some companies that downsized in panic are now forced to rehire. They are now taking on two part-timers instead of one full-timer. Such part-timers are easier to find, require fewer benefits, and appear to be more industrious when working for shorter periods. Older part-timers can hack the shorter day, whereas they may be pushing it to go back full-time.

Others in the over-sixty-five age group have started new businesses, such as delivering a two-week supply of frozen packaged meals to those over eighty-five, now the fastest growing segment of the adult population. These older people are still healthy, but constant shopping and preparing food is a bit much. With this service and a microwave they can enjoy proper nutrition with minimum effort. I could use this service myself. One woman in Hudson, Indiana, grossed $55,000 in one month from her six hundred clients.

One of the easiest opportunities, but one that requires an alert mind, is the business of information brokering. Executives require summaries of trade journal and other articles related to their work. They simply don't have time to read everything that is happening. Working retirees skim everything and provide customers with a condensed version. It does require computer literacy to acquire the speed and breadth of information needed. And an in-depth knowledge of the industry you have just left is, of course, a great help.

Is there life after retirement? You bet. It's called work.

→   *The End of Unions*

From 1910 until well into the 1930s, labor unions, especially in the United States, grew at record rates. For the first time since the formation of guilds in Europe between the twelfth and eighteenth centuries, common workers were able to assemble in massive unions for protection against the practices of huge companies, mainly those in the production-line manufacturing of products or in coal mining. John L. Lewis, the militant and dominant labor boss who was elected president of the United Mine Workers of America in 1920, controlled 300,000 well paid coal workers across America, the majority in the anthracite coal mines of Pennsylvania.

The demands of John L. Lewis for higher wages for his hard-working miners (usually obtained by long, bitter strikes during cold winters when coal was the basic heat source) may have inadvertently ignited the spark that exploded the dormant powder keg of technology, whose force is still spreading in ever-widening circles around the planet.

As a direct result of a series of strikes, coal-mine owners, seeing the eventual failure of their mines due to high labor costs, started what has developed into the research and development movement of today. One of the first big payoffs was the automatic coal miner – a mechanical monster with whirling horizontal, then vertical, then fully pivoting blades – that could mine a vein of coal dozens of times faster than pick-and-shovel miners could. In a short time, during the Depression of the 1930s and the universal introduction of the automatic coal miner, the United Mine Workers lost half its members. The price of coal dropped, and mining efficiency and consumption of coal went up, until union strength was no longer a major blockade to production. That also started the end of the glory days of anthracite coal mining. World War II and the rapid search for, and development of, oil fields produced a more easily handled and transported fuel. Coal went out of fashion. With the exception of workers at open-pit mining of the less fuel-efficient bituminous coal, mined with even higher productivity because of technology, the previously dominant mining union faded.

The same pattern is visible in the logging industry today. Technology in the form of the mechanical "tree-farmer" now requires no timber-topper, the highly paid lumberjack who did the dangerous job of topping a tree and then swaying back and forth until the cut portion crashed to the ground. Huge radio-advised bulldozers with blades, mechanical arms, and massive winches and saws now convert trees to logs in minutes.

Today one skilled operator can do the work of several dozen workers, and the transported tree moves automatically through a computer-controlled sawmill at a speed that makes the whole process look like magic. Highly paid computer operators (some from the ranks of early computer "nerds") now chalk up salaries of $100,000 annually. In one modernized plant, I noticed that the crew in the computer operations room were still wearing the traditional blue shirts of their counterparts of yesterday.

That intrigued me. When I looked closer I could see that they were blue, all right, but made of silk. When I investigated further I found that these workers went to an in-house school one day a week to learn how to keep up to the increasing intellectual demands of their new positions. Meanwhile, the head of one west coast woodworkers' union admits that 40 percent of his remaining members are illiterate.

Today technology makes the laws and breaks the laws, civil, moral, and economic. If you keep up with change, the future is ever bright. Stick with the past, the old ways, and things not only look awful and demoralizing, they will be. Similar changes to those in mining and forestry are happening on the factory floor, in department stores, and offices. The labor union as we know it is doomed.

→ *Universal Language*

Some years ago researchers found that we can control our mental alpha and beta waves by directing our thoughts. This control was used mainly for meditation and relaxation. We have since learned to use such "thought waves" in conjunction with certain switching devices to control and command computers. For the past ten years I have been using such a "hippie headband" device to turn my computer on or off, run a program, or instruct the printer to print. It may not be much at the moment, but neither is a child at conception.

Here is what I think will shortly be possible. We all have thought waves. The signals are very weak; however, there has been rapid increase in amplification techniques in a dozen fields. For example, a device, reduced by modern technology to the size of a hearing aid, could soon be planted in my ear. It would contain an amplifier modeled after the low noise amplifier now used in almost all satellite dishes. There the amplifier takes the very weak signal received from a communications satellite hovering over the equator at an altitude of 22,300 miles, and it increases the volume and the picture signal perhaps 200,000 times. Now imagine this for the future. You wake up one morning wondering what to do. You remember, "Oh yes, today I was going to run Program 7001," a landscaping program. There is this device in your ear that can amplify the thought wave signal two million times. The hearing unit passes on that amplified thought wave via an infrared signal (similar to what you now use for your TV) to your "smart" bulldozer outside. The bulldozer's memory unit contains Program 7001, so it starts up – and moves that mountain. Untouched by human hands.

For years people have claimed they can see auras. Russian Kirlian photography showed that every person emits an energy force. These unknowns are to the mindlink era what radio and television waves were to the early industrial world.

Fujitsu, Japan's largest computer company, now has a "universal translator," which translates Japanese into English and vice versa at a thousand words a minute. A video I play at many seminars shows a Kenyan speaking Swahili from Japan via satellite to a Canadian Inuit in the Northwest Territories who replies in Inuktitut.

Using the translation program, the people speaking different languages can understand one another. Since the dialogue has been digitized it can also be voice-synthesized. Think of the implications for international business. What will it do to translators in a bilingual country such as Canada, or at the United Nations? What will it do to school boards and countries that have scheduled billions of dollars for language training? Will anyone want to learn another language when there is no longer any financial incentive to do so?

3

Future Business

→ *The Third Market*

In a changing world, retailers have a choice. Set nets for the well-heeled, who are fussy, demand top service, and want the best – this is where the highest per individual sale profit resides. This is the first market. Or else deal with that segment of the market that makes most of its decisions on price alone. That's the second market.

Today there is a new kid at the counter, the third market, better known as the entrepreneurial movement. It might yet save America. In times when large companies are shrinking like cheap shirts and laying off staff, when such giants don't know how or where to move or how to play the much faster business game, why are there a million small American companies growing at an annual rate of 15 percent?

How have the huge companies, which once had all those markets tied up, got into such a fix? What have they to offer now, when all their executives who have spent their lives learning to play business/baseball have nothing to offer but the same old, worn-out products and poor service? Why can't they learn the new, much faster game of business/jai alai? The same reason an elephant with arthritis can't out-run a gazelle.

These small companies are producing 44 percent of all business-to-business sales, according to a report prepared for Wilson L. Harrell, former publisher of *Inc.* magazine. Eighty percent of all new jobs created during the past decade have come through the actions of these entrepreneurial companies. Some have grown at lightning speed. With products and services for the Information Age there is often little relationship between cost and selling price, so profit margins border on the magnificent.

In the software field, once development costs have been covered, the actual cost of reproducing software copies – whether on computer programs, disk books, CD-ROM, audiotapes or videotapes – resides in the minimal wholesale costs of a disk ($.19 to $.35) or a tape ($.50 to $10), and packaging ($.50 to $10). Retail price can run from $20 to $5,000, depending on what the product can do for you. Almost always the product is price insensitive. It is usually better and quicker and costs less than whatever it is replacing. People, at least for now, are so impressed with comparisons with the past (computer vs. typewriter, ultra-compactness vs. bulk, speed vs. snail mail, brainpower vs. muscle power) that price, once consumers understand what the new product or service can do, becomes a fourth or fifth priority.

Will some larger companies see the writing on the screen and follow these leaders of relatively small businesses to success? The General Business Systems Division of AT&T is converting some of its branches into franchises! IBM, admittedly belatedly, chopped a fifth of its Canadian operation and one hundred thousand employees from its staff worldwide to survive. Not only is IBM now a much better company, it provides better service.

These are not isolated cases. It is happening everywhere. Globalization means competition can come from anywhere – and everywhere. Like it or not, it's this sense of urgency that drives the successful – here or in Kuala Lumpur.

→ *Nuggets*
Amid Chaos

Whenever decisions are made amid massive change, panic, or chaos, some turn out to be faulty. These may include the divesting by corporations under stress of once-promising research and development projects because they would not produce profit in time to solve an immediate monetary crisis. Opportunities get ignored when corporate resources are in short supply. Decision makers may be so wrapped up in attempting to save the ship that they fail to notice a more viable vessel drifting by.

Forty percent of the Fortune 500 big names of a decade ago no longer exist. Some of their patents, projects, products, and the debris from their collapse could be updated, modified, or re-invented for today's marketplace. In some cases the market now could make a winner out of yesteryear's loser – for an entrepreneur ready to take advantage of the situation.

Look at what's happening with office space. Most cities are experiencing an abundance of empty buildings because of corporate downsizing, reductions in the numbers of employees and space formerly required to operate in the corporate playground. Around the world, this vacancy rate, as reported by local boards of trade and real estate organizations, is running around 20 percent. The true figure is probably closer to 30 percent because many larger companies have downsized from, say, three to two floors in an office complex and now have a floor empty, which doesn't show up in the real estate statistics.

This space is transparent. No one sees it but the company trying to sublet it. Building owners want to rent their own empty space, not space belonging to some responsible company they have on the

45

hook for another five or ten years. The company subletting is a little embarrassed that it doesn't need what its top executives decided some time ago would be necessary for the next decade. Education and experience never taught them to prepare for surprises. The next surprise they hear may be personally more fatal: "Sorry, but we have to let you go. Corporate restructuring, you know."

That's the dark view. Let's look at the opportunity. As fewer and fewer people go into a city to work in emptying office towers, they work from home. Their office space has already been built: it was the den, now converted to a far more productive office. No additional structural investment or rent is required. New work-at-home equipment (appliances for productivity) must be installed, but at minimal cost, since the necessary wires connecting them to the world of cyberspace generally are already in place.

Less gas is used as rush-hour traffic drops when fewer people drive downtown. That means less pollution, fewer accidents, and lower car insurance premiums. Suburban traffic and rural traffic will increase slightly, but those roads never had a full load. Not only do transportation costs drop dramatically, but such things as dry cleaning and fancy clothing bills also shrink. Expensive restaurant lunches and at least a portion of daycare payments can also be saved.

The more stationary workplace means more traffic from package delivery or mail-order companies and less business for downtown office suppliers. This creates still more empty space and reduces office rental rates, although not enough to compete with work-at-home rents several magnitudes lower.

What happens to urban planners? Some cities have hundreds of expensive planners on staff trying to create a crisis they can sell to the public: "We must preserve our green space. Roads will be gridlocked in ten years. Our cherished values will disappear." Not so. Technology will make many of today's problems vanish. Need I repeat all those worries from the past that somehow disappeared? Nuclear conflagration, oil shortages, global warming, etc.

Don't react emotionally to planners' dreams. They cannot predict what will happen in times of rapid change. They are simply trying to save their own jobs now that a more enlightened and sophisticated public is asking embarrassing questions. We are not on the *Titanic*. We haven't hit an iceberg. The universe will continue to unfold.

But there will be surprises. Ask planners, "What surprises have you built into your model?" Have they considered the effect on agricultural land when biotechnology allows a three-story, five-acre building to grow more produce than a two-hundred-acre farm? Have they considered the changes in value of their precious farmland by the introduction of the new Boeing 747-400 cargo series jet? Have they considered what happens when Japanese companies open food factories in northern China where there is plenty of cheap land, fresh water, and skilled farm labor available for $1 a day? With the new cargo jets, food harvested in the morning in China can be delivered to North America the same day. The Dutch have been doing this for a decade. Flowers picked in the early morning in The Netherlands are delivered in New York the same afternoon – at half the cost.

Technology today makes the laws and breaks the laws. Planners have problems anticipating what the next invention or innovation will be, so they are unable to cover the exigencies that will modify social structure. Today the only effective planning is training for change. The best five-year planning belonged to the U.S.S.R. and General Motors. Where did it get them?

→   *Outsourcing*

Yesterday and tomorrow live side by side in Plano, Texas. Alongside a field containing a few grazing buffalo lies another field formerly known for its corn. Today it holds the largest private digital/fiber-optic/satellite communications network in the world, EDS. The control room makes the one at the Space Shuttle's Mission Control look like a covered wagon. Here there is, according to *USA Today*, "enough computing power to balance 5.4 billion checkbooks – one

47

for every person in the world – in one second." There are also robot magnetic tape switchers that make thirty-five thousand physical transactions in a day!

EDS was formerly Electronic Data Systems, Inc. of Dallas, Texas. It was created by legendary and charismatic founder H. Ross Perot, who sold out – for a reported $742.8 million in cash – to General Motors in 1984, after telling GM Chairman Roger Smith he wasn't running the business very well. It appears to have been a win-win sale. It made Perot a billionaire, and EDS has since exploded into a $7-billion a year empire, just like Apple Corporation, which is now both a vendor and a client to EDS. Roger Smith, who couldn't change fast enough with the times, is now long gone from GM.

What kind of business is EDS? Once upon a time companies and municipalities thought they could do everything on their own. In the Industrial Age this was possible. Cities, towns, and villages collected their own garbage, cleaned their own buildings, towed their own parking violators, repaired their own streets, and ran their own jails and police and fire departments. Companies did the same in their fields.

Then both cities and companies found that other organizations that concentrated on only collecting the garbage or repairing the streets, or handling telemarketing, video production, tax accounting, or computer processing were capable of doing a better job for less money. Companies found there were tax advantages, too, like not depreciating your own trucks over long periods of time but being able to write off immediately the monthly fee charged by the contractor. They also no longer had the headache of running their own, sometimes touchy, computer mainframe staff. As well, because some of these companies purchase in greater quantities, they found they had purchasing clout and hence received a better price from the service provider. Today the whole process is called "outsourcing." EDS is the world's largest outsource in the communications field.

According to *USA Today,* "One in every twenty Fortune 500 companies uses computer service companies such as EDS. By 1993 one in every five companies will need an outside computer service company's help, and EDS should be the largest benefactor."

Here's how it works. EDS visits your company, finds out what you are trying to accomplish, and provides the latest equipment and the best communications system to link your many systems, all over the world if necessary, rolling everything into one seamless operation. Since it does not manufacture any computer or other hardware equipment itself (it does create software), EDS has no built-in bias. It is the world's largest user of IBM mainframes (over one hundred of them), but it also uses Apple, or other computer hardware, choosing the best available to solve any particular need. Can you imagine the price that EDS staffers get when they deal? Nobody, but nobody can compete. And if they don't like the quoted price they can go elsewhere.

EDS must be doing something right. Since 1984 the company has grown from $750 million a year gross to today's $7.1 billion. It has over seven thousand customers and about 70,500 employees in eighty countries. It enters into leases as long as ten years with clients. When you sign on with EDS, it will usually purchase the equipment you have on hand and, in many cases, hire all your present staff. To show you how much superior training EDS staff obtains and your ex-staff will receive, the company spends $100 million a year on training. One in every five EDS employees is a systems engineer. Only one in every 2,300 other employees is a lawyer. What is that saying?

When I view a company like EDS, I look for what's creative behind the large numbers. I found that EDS had won a five-year, $400-million contract in Chicago to solve that city's parking ticket problem. It seems that Chicago was one year in arrears in keying into its computers a backlog of twenty-four million parking tickets. First, that showed me at least that EDS was finding necessary business clues and then converting those clues into contracts.

Other competitors were on the Chicago trail, but only EDS came up with a sample presentation using hand-held personal computers that would issue tickets and transfer the data to the city's computer each day. This was one more sign of innovative thinking. The most common excuse for not paying a ticket in Chicago has been the claim that the Windy City winds had blown tickets away before the drivers returned to their vehicles. The EDS proposal included tickets with an adhesive.

EDS also provided an electronic imaging system that can produce an image of the ticket on a computer screen. This enables the city to hold neighborhood hearings instead of using costly court time. Before EDS took over, only 10 percent of the tickets were paid within a year (remember, the city was a year behind in issuing such tickets). Now it's up to 47 percent and climbing. Revenues from parking violations are expected to increase 62 percent in 1993 to more than $60 million. EDS obviously did what the city could not do by itself, and justice is no longer denied by being delayed.

EDS is a self-operating subsidiary of General Motors. Once 70 percent of its total billings were with the parent company. This has dropped to below 50 percent as new, independent outsourcing business became the growth market. It's a business with a bright future.

→ *Electronic Labor*

In an age of instant round-the-world-communications, old thoughts, old possibilities, and apparently stable procedures become subject to rapid change. Today it is not the raw materials and the manufacturing plants that are essential. It is the information about a product or service that is most important.

Production costs of hardware and software are high in North America because of our high wages. The blunt fact is that now that we have to compete with the world we are overpaid and we under-produce. In the rest of the world almost all costs are lower. And we are naive if we think others can't do it just as well and at lower cost. It was only a matter of time until labor was "imported" electronically. That day has dawned.

In a small way this has been happening for some time. Some North American companies started years ago to send keyboard punching operations overseas, mainly to the Caribbean, where wage rates for the dull, routine jobs were a fraction of what had to be paid in North America.

CyberSoft in the Philippines, via its North American marketing base in San Francisco, offers computer data entry. Prices start at seventy-five cents per thousand computer keystrokes, with a guaranteed accuracy rate of 99.95 percent. That kind of proficiency is not available in North America. In the Philippines most jobs become a matter of living. Workers force themselves to learn more, faster, and to make no mistakes. That makes them competitive in a world looking for the right attitude. CyberSoft has learned how to make this attractive to North American software developers and other companies looking for low-cost data entry. This company has more than two hundred highly educated and well-trained personnel, providing an inexpensive long-distance work force. CyberSoft is progressing beyond straight data entry. Need a map digitized? Technical manuals, geological well logs, or medical journal inputted? This company is doing it all.

China too is entering this field with rates running between three and eight cents a page for data inputting. China has a unique system that puts two people on the project. Both input simultaneously. Then a cross-checking software program similar to a spelling checker catches any differences.

Computer programming is another area of electronically imported labor. Software developers have found high-grade programmers elsewhere – at twenty cents for every U.S. dollar. Overseas programmers were first used in England, where competent programmers were available at half the cost of their North American counterparts. A larger labor source is now India. Eastern Systems Technology of Madras has set up a U.S. subsidiary in California to sell offshore software development. A second Indian company, Raba Contell of New Delhi, has also entered the field.

Although foreign competition might also come from Singapore, Hong Kong, or even Japan, the lack of a language barrier is India's big advantage. Many of those involved in India have been educated in the United States or Canada. They know the requirements here, according to Ram Mani, president of Eastern Systems, a computer science graduate of Stanford University and a Silicon Valley consultant for the past eight years. Experienced software engineers can live in India on a fraction of what they would be paid in North America. An Indian software engineer with three to five years' experience and a master's degree makes less than $1,000 a month but can enjoy a luxurious lifestyle on that income.

In Palo Alto a small three-year-old company operating out of a cottage attached to a garage is electronically importing software programmers from Moscow right into the heart of Silicon Valley. How did it happen? Michael DeLyon, a San Francisco area financial analyst, one day had a problem. He couldn't finish a computer program for a client. He knew he was in trouble as he was short of cash at the time and couldn't hire the high-priced local help. What to do? Call "program busters" in Moscow. In Moscow? Yes. DeLyon shipped his inoperative software to a friend in Moscow who returned it via fax. Problem solved. Client happy. Business born.

Today, DeLyon's company brings together American companies with software cost problems and skilled eastern European software programmers who feel rich on a quarter of the going rate for such work in North America. Now InterContinental Software has six hundred foreign workers on standby ready to work on a contract basis. In knowledge industries, brainpower is the only raw material. Eastern Europe, always strong in math and sciences, has these resources by the town-full, and at a bargain price by our standards.

Selling the idea does take time, according to DeLyon. U.S. companies aren't quick to take the bait, but when they see they can reduce costs by 75 percent they realize that if they don't and others do, they are out of business. Even with such talent at low cost, DeLyon still has competition – from India, Great Britain, Hungary, and China. I myself have been approached by universities in Nigeria offering to do such programming at even lower cost. But InterContinental Software claims to offer quality, the biggest selling feature in today's marketplace. "We are the wave of the future," DeLyon says. "I'm now ready to tackle Canada."

Although importing labor electronically poses still another threat to North American employment levels, it also promises an eventual drop in the price of software as such savings filter down the supply pipeline. It also shows that a new type of thinking will shortly be in big demand here.

→ ## Are Buildings Obsolete?

The period from 1865 to 1890 was the age of the railroad building spree across North America. Everyone got into the act. The iron horse helped open up North America in a manner never before possible, propelling new immigrants westward and economically upward to undreamed-of heights. Shortly after Ford and rubber tires appeared, the railways began to fade.

The period from 1975 to 1990 was the age of the building spree around the world. The volume of office, retail, industrial, and even residential floor space reached unheard-of levels. The building boom, along with the construction of the necessary supporting infrastructure, propelled most earthlings to new levels of affluence, even in many developing countries. Could buildings, as we have known them, also vanish in the years to come?

All trends suggest the answer is yes. Look at office space. Sydney, Australia, known for never having a vacancy rate above 5 percent, saw vacancy rates shoot up from 2 to 11 percent between 1990 and 1992. In Toronto, vacancies were already at 11.9 percent when another 10.3 million square feet of office space came on stream in 1991. With the Ontario economy reeling from the depression,

53

investors reluctant to make new investments because of recent legislation, and threatening suggestions coming from the socialist New Democratic Party government, office vacancy rates will increase further, perhaps to more than 20 percent.

In the United States, real estate excesses have reached new heights. Everyone thought being "King of the Hill" was a great, lucrative, exciting game. Look at the picture today: of the thirty top commercial real estate markets in the United States, twenty have vacancy rates higher than 15 percent. One source says the true current vacancy rate in Los Angeles is 25 percent! Houston and other oil patch cities are running around a quarter empty. *Global Finance* magazine quotes Daniel Neidich of Goldman Sachs as predicting that "vacancies won't be low enough to attract new development for another eight or nine years."

If that sounds bad, look at London, England, where vacancy rates are now at 15 percent, a record in almost any European city. Rents have dropped 35 percent to $29 a square foot, and both rents and vacancy rates look as if they will move lower as surviving lessees seek ways to cut costs. The world's biggest landlord, Canada's Olympia & York Corporation, is under bankruptcy protection in New York, London, and at home in Toronto.

In Tokyo, rents have dropped 20 percent, although vacancy rates still hover between the official figure of around 1 percent and the "street rating" of 5 percent. In a country where bank interest ran around 3.5 percent when U.S. rates were galloping along at 10 percent, it is quite a shock to find that this makes a big difference. Now that Japanese interest rates have risen, predictions of a drop in real estate values of up to 30 percent have already come true.

An even bigger shock to global confidence comes from Switzerland, where bank real estate loans total SFr 363.7 billion and total bank equity is only SFr 67.3 billion. Here a rise in office vacancies could trigger commercial space bankruptcies with a rise in uncollectible mortgage building loans. This has the potential to trigger a domino effect throughout the Swiss banking establishment.

All cities keep track of their vacant commercial and office space. What they do not keep a record of is "invisible vacancies." As mentioned, these are the spaces that become vacant when corporations downsize and put their entire operation on, say, two floors instead of four. They still pay rent for that vacant space, which does not show up on any official record.

I suggest that these vacancies could add as much as 10 percent to a city's official vacancy rate. This will eventually show up in the sluggish rental of existing visible vacancies, because the original renters of "invisible vacancies" are willing to offer rental at almost any price. It will also draw potential lessees away from the building owners' rental office because the tenants with space to sublet are desperate to make a deal.

The trend may even accelerate as new, unbelievably compact optical storage systems reduce the amount of required storage space. Two floors out of every thirteen in any office tower are occupied with storing manila file folders. With the average floor comprised of 10,000 square feet that adds up to a lot of money, around $1 million for the two floors. All that data can now be stored on one SERODS (Surface Enhanced Raman Optical Data Storage) disk – one 12-inch disk!

And on top of all this is the trend toward small businesses that operate from the home. One recent survey from Canada says that 25 percent of the Canadian work force is now doing some work at home. All indications are that this trend will continue, adding another damper on the rental of traditional office space.

In the nineteenth century we overbuilt railway lines and railroad rolling stock. Have we overbuilt fixed capital building assets in the fading days of the twentieth century? Could wealth held in fixed assets go through a devaluation similar to that of the German mark after World War I?

→　　　*Life at City Hall*

The Industrial Age compartmentalized everything and life was relatively simple. You had a place to live, a place to work, a place to play, and even places to eat (other than your home). The zoning process kept everything neat and tidy, just like your front lawn was supposed to be. Get ready for chaos.

Almost all cities now have a problem with illegal suites (apartments) – people aren't following the rules anymore, for apparently sound reasons. The growing list of court rulings against any "discriminatory" actions does not carry clout. People are no longer terrorized by bureaucracy (if anything, it's the other way around). It makes it tough to get the populace to proceed the way bureaucrats had planned (usually without getting anyone else's opinion).

In North America at least 10 percent of the working population (i.e., taxpayers) are working at home. In almost every residential district that is technically illegal. It will get worse (or better, depending on the point of view). Thanks to modern technological devices (most small, highly efficient, capable of worldwide hookups), many new sunrise industries can operate in very small quarters with a surprisingly small staff. In many cases the staff doesn't even have to be at the same location as the official office; they telecommute via phone lines. Such companies increasingly show a growth rate double that of sunset-industry companies. They have lower overhead, show larger per-employee dollar sales, and look at the world as their market. And for more progressive companies that treat workers as partners or shareholders, the workers themselves will be continually looking for ways to increase company sales and keep costs down.

What are the implications for big-city real estate? Now that it is unnecessary to pay $30 a square foot to store manila folders, won't space requirements drop? Will the large hierarchy of staff required in the Industrial Age not decrease dramatically as workers, using the latest equipment, become more productive? Think what this will mean to those "easy" taxes paid in one lump from large real estate holding companies. Now city hall has to handle more of the smaller trade.

Even the definition of work takes on new meaning. Back in the 1930s work was mainly physical. Computers and most of our other new toys didn't exist then. Fifty percent of current goods and services didn't exist even five years ago. Ninety percent of all you will work or play with by the start of the third millennium hasn't yet been developed.

City Hall will have trouble during the next decade supporting many bylaws now on the books. Let's look at manufacturing. I turn newspaper columns into books – not Gutenberg style, where you can see and feel them, but electronic books. Is that "working"? I sell books but I duplicate my master electronically on a 3.5-inch disk and mail it out. Is that "manufacturing"? If so, I'll send it electronically over the phone – that can't be manufacturing. I can make motion pictures with color and sound on my Apple Macintosh II computer. Does that make me a television studio?

City Hall will become overwhelmed by the volume and complexity of future business. The world is now globalized. Any business can move almost anywhere. How will cities react to the prospect of losing the dynamic entrepreneurship of their brightest and most job-creating citizens? The budget crunches of the '90s are nothing compared to what our municipal politicians will have to deal with in the next century.

→ *Desktop*
 Manufacturing

When I first mentioned desktop publishing fifteen years ago, I was considered a kook. A few years later, when I wrote about desktop video, people were skeptical but showed some interest. Get ready for desktop manufacturing.

Here is how it works. Computer-created designs can be electronically transferred to a "box," a machine that converts the designs to pass through a laser beam that "cures" a liquid plastic inside the box and converts the on-screen design almost immediately into a solid, three-dimensional object. The process originally was designed to make models of a product more quickly than those made by the earlier, partially computerized process.

Right now on my computer console stands one of the first samples from that machine, a perfume bottle for Avon. Hundreds of other products have been zapped out in the past couple of years. What used to take five years can now take, with the latest technology, less than one. What used to be done with one machine to make models can now be done with a single computer, hooked up to ten, a hundred, or a thousand machines. This is desktop manufacturing. In other words, workerless factories.

Old-style factory jobs are obsolete. Single-worker companies, task forces, and small, owner-operated companies will be the financially viable units of tomorrow. This change will mean horrendous problems for governments. No longer will the major portion of government revenues come from large corporations. Governments will have to deal with thousands of small, almost insignificant, companies, that together will provide much of the wealth of the country. Even politicians will be hard hit. Instead of receiving a few huge political contributions for their election campaigns, they will have to gather countless small donations. Union contributions are already shrinking as unions lose members and become more independent, no longer donating a portion of dues for political action but leaving such political donations up to individual members.

With modern communications and ultrasmart manufacturing equipment able to operate almost on its own intelligence, the whole concept of manufacturing takes on new meaning. The value of software today is rapidly surpassing the value of hardware as we have known it in the past. Software is usually provided by knowledge workers working alone or in very small teams. When the software is perfected, and after research and development costs have been written off, profit margins sometimes reach 75 percent or higher. It takes only seconds to duplicate any knowledge program and computer disks cost pennies. Before long, anyone with a desktop will be able to get into the manufacturing business.

→   *Business Link*

A company called Business Link Communications uses all forms of communications, messengers, couriers, and standard E-mail modems. But it keeps pushing the envelope. And it's threatening to blow its competitors out of the water. Operating around the clock, 364 days a year, Business Link can now do a job in Vancouver or Vienna faster than a resident competitor in either city. This may sound unusual but it soon won't be. Their success signals what will occur in virtually every industry that persists in doing "business as usual."

Business Link can complete almost any high-quality printing job in three hours (the company calls that "standard"). A rush job takes one hour (extra charge). Compare this with your printer's time schedule. In Manhattan, the company's fleet of foot and bike messengers delivers *free* around the clock. Delivery anywhere else in North America and fifteen other countries is overnight.

In addition to any four-color printing job – high quality at reasonable prices – the company offers remote on-screen proofing of artwork, remote technical support, and on-line access to designers' portfolios at multiple sites. Access to the company's bulletin board system for high-speed downloading of font libraries, logos, and utilities is also part of the service. Using such a top-notch service allows you to control a major printing operation from the other side of the continent. Who can compete with that?

The speed of the new system is phenomenal, especially in the publishing business. Clients can transmit material at the rate of one megabyte in three minutes direct to their "instant" image-setting facility. This replaces slow modems, messengers, couriers, and systems that used to take days or weeks. The company uses the universal switched 56,000 wide-area network, which enables it to send and receive files twenty-three times faster than the 2400 bps via analog modems. Business Link transmits in three minutes what takes others an hour. Now any desktop publisher can compete with anyone in the world – by dealing with such a new-style production printing operator.

Business Link is using the latest technology to give superior service. Their competitors are still debating if they really want to spend all that money on new, in many cases untried, technology. This is the age of the risk-taker. While you debate the issue, someone else is preparing to steal your customers.

→   *Voicewriter*

Robotronics – automation in an advanced form – has been most effective on the factory floor, mainly in the automotive field. Now comes the first major assault on the office. Kurzweil AI (Artificial Intelligence) of Los Angeles has been building an impressive record during the past ten years. The Kurzweil music synthesizer developed under research director and pioneer Robert Moog has astounded music critics with an advanced digital keyboard instrumentation able to reproduce every acoustical instrument and electronic sound. It is literally changing the sound of music. Kurzweil's "Reading Machine for the Blind" is the world's first character recognition system capable of handling virtually any ordinary type style. It may be a bigger advance than braille.

Now the Kurzweil AI Voicesystem replaces the most important office ingredient – the secretary. This innovation will change the office drastically. The executive can dictate directly to an office television set. Built-in software will correct spelling and punctuation and move paragraphs around. A spoken word dispatches the letter at the speed of light to the addressee, usually at a cost less than current postage (especially if sent by the upcoming National Information Utility "Moon Mail"). This innovation will replace at one stroke many office stenographers, secretaries, and mail rooms.

For three years I tested the "Voice Entry Terminal" made by the Scott Instrument Company of Denton, Texas. One of the first in the field, this unit worked fine but had a very limited vocabulary. Now Kurzweil has moved into this market with a thousand-word vocabulary of your choice in a self-contained desktop unit. First applications are expected in the fields of medical reporting, Computer-aided Design/Computer-aided Manufacturing (CAD/CAM) command and control, voice mail, basic dictation, and remote inquiry to computer data banks.

Coming soon is the Kurzweil Voicewriter with a ten-thousand-word vocabulary. With optical storage reducing the need for paper filing and the Voicewriter reducing secretarial office staff, the question will soon be: Is an office even necessary?

→   *The Voice Mail
    Backlash*

I have a general bias in favor of technology, yet some technologies create more trouble than benefits, almost from their introduction. Voice mail is a prime example. At a time when customer and supplier service is paramount, voice mail is the run-around, hassle-ridden, pot-holed, gravel road of the Communications Age. The voice-mail time-waster first explains, usually in lengthy terms, how to leave a message. A voice rattles off instructions faster than some people can follow, and tells you to push a number to contact the person you were trying to reach – often because that person wanted to talk to you and left you a message yesterday!

Meanwhile (especially galling on long distance calls) it tells you to wait, leave a message (which was all you were trying to do in the first place), or press unknown digits, the value of which no one has explained. This is inconvenient to the caller, and potentially damaging to the people/company using the voice-mail system. They risk losing clients, customers, and/or suppliers.

The caller gets the impression that the instigators of the system consider their time more important than anyone else's. You peasants and outsiders can follow instructions. Leave your message, if you are bright enough to figure out how, and someone may call you back. Perhaps after a half-hour coffee break with other Stone-Age employees.

I usually put in a busy day. Yet I answer all calls personally unless I am out of town. The caller wastes no time, my answer is immediate, and both of us can get on to the next matter at hand. If I am out of town, I check messages and get back to callers. Constantly recycling two people's time to make it more convenient for voice-mail receivers is wasteful.

My suggestion is this. If voice mail bugs you as much as it bugs me, hang up as soon as you recognize a voice-mail system. Let them call you back. After all, they already called you once. Your time is as valuable as theirs. And don't be bashful – let them know what you think of a company that uses such a system. They are probably making other transparent mistakes as well.

Every new technology has social implications. In the case of voice mail it is already converting dissatisfied phone users into ardent fax advocates. Send a fax instead – no waiting, message delivered. Perhaps a "telephone hour" will evolve, when people will personally answer phone calls at a pre-announced time, say 0900–1000 daily, Monday to Friday. Callers who expect a call back should know when they plan to be there to answer the phone.

→   *Office-Pool Robots*

Automation hit the factory floor with faster methods of handling materials and machines. In the process, much of the dirty, dangerous, heavy, or monotonous work previously handled by humans was eliminated. Some of these machines were called robots. The first generation of robots, which were unable to see, feel, or think, are already taking early retirement (without any pension checks). They are being replaced by robots that can see and, to a certain degree, think. But the life span of these new metal drones will not be long either.

Third-generation robots, with built-in artificial intelligence, are already on the drawing board. Workerless factories will become commonplace. A few such factories exist already in both the United States (Whirlpool washers) and Japan (Fanuc). "What's that got to do with me?" you ask. "I work in an office. Robots can never replace the human touch in my workplace. Brains, not microchips, will always be needed there."

Wrong. Automation in the office is here now. Real automation. A few humans will always be needed, of course, operating in new positions at the executive level, perhaps akin to the communications managers of today. But thousands of stenographic and secretarial positions will be replaced by technoscribes.

This new position will result from a dramatic upgrading of old secretarial skills and differ from the workerless factory, in that one human works with the latest computer techniques and a company's best thinkers. It is the brainchild of Bernie Dekoven of Playworks! Inc., a computing group in Palo Alto, California. The technoscribe is the key element in what Dekoven terms "computer-enhanced meetings."

The new technique creates a new meeting environment, in which a Macintosh computer is fed data from the discussions at a meeting. It almost instantaneously provides charts, graphs, scales, idea formats, etc., which speed up the meeting and allow participants to see far beyond what might have gone on in a conventional meeting.

Think of having the results of your meeting during the meeting! That is the advantage of having a technoscribe. Of course, the technoscribe doesn't have to be in the office. Nor does any of the creative team: they can be at home. Interconnected by terminals, team members could teleconference just as efficiently from anywhere in the world and receive reports of the meeting while it's still in progress.

4

The Everyday World

→ *The Shape of*
Things to Come

"Ceramic-home living certainly makes life a lot easier than when your dad and I moved into our first home," said Ms. Nanton to her daughter. "Who would have thought that a house could be smarter and have a better memory than your father!"

Farfetched? Such comments may not be unusual as we enter the third millennium. Homes guaranteed for more than twenty years, with no fire insurance (because they are made of silicon and limestone) and carrying a lower mortgage rate (because the financial lending institution can't lose) will be common. These homes will automatically equalize humidity levels with the outside air when you take a shower. They will turn up the heat an hour before a cold wave hits your district. Such homes will still have the refrigerator in the kitchen but the motor for that fridge (and that irritating buzzing sound) will be in the garage, where the heat it produces will keep your car from freezing.

Of course the house will adjust each room as you enter for your thermal comfort level. Personal identity sensors will adjust to you, your partner, or the kids, depending on who is in the room. If everyone appears simultaneously, it will average or follow any specific pre-programmed command for such occasions. And the house automatically turns on your personal computer/robot education/information/entertainment holographic image projector in what will quickly grow to be the favorite room in the house. This is the residence of the knowledge navigator, your at-home-learning computer directed by an Apple-developed system that "understands" how you think.

A project known as America, Part II will have a dramatic effect on our way of life and the way we perceive learning. The philosophy behind it says: if we can throw a switch for electricity and turn a tap for water, why can't we just hit a button for knowledge? A substantial portion of time previously spent watching TV entertainment will be converted into a learning process by building a high "interest factor" into shows, as is done now for commercials, sitcoms, and the evening news. Learning will become increasingly visual as it becomes obvious that static book knowledge cannot compete with dynamic visual information. Many people will have difficulty accepting this change: old habits are not automatically eradicated when the rules of life change suddenly.

New forms of visual entertainment on a grand scale will appear. Large enclosed stadiums and convention centers will offer high-definition images on huge flat/curved screens, giving the impression that viewers are physically involved in the performance. (The beginnings of such developments are already evident in places like the SkyDome in Toronto, with its Jumbotron scoreboard.) Massive productions will be created at unbelievable cost for the one live production, recorded holographically. Such shows will be relayed via satellite, or more likely fiber-optic cables, to world centers for presentation in large arenas to huge audiences willing to pay $100 or more per viewing. "Nostalgia" theaters will continue to be supported by the older, more conventional segment of society, just as they are today. They will be accepted as the visual museums of yesterday.

Obviously, those who live in smart houses won't put up with dumb cars. Many homes will have built-in natural gas and electric recharging units for "smart cars." Before the end of the twentieth century most cars will have microwave ovens next to the glove compartment. New "Heat & Eat" packaged foods will be sold at natural gas/electric recharging service stations. Most will carry the Campbell's Soup label as Campbell's research, under way since 1988, will give the company an "out front" image. Such cars will also contain sensors that keep us just twenty-five feet behind the car ahead. From other sensors farther along on the highway, the car will "know" of obstacles or slowing traffic that will require gradual braking. Such sensors will standardize traffic flow, permitting a 50 percent increase in the number of cars on the road with fewer traffic jams than today. Dashboard-projected video (DPV) will allow the driver to read all speed and other instruments without taking his or her eyes off the road.

Permanently installed low-cost phones will serve as a back-up to your personal, wrist-implanted phone. This will be the fourth generation of the compact cordless phone introduced in Britain in 1989. Even then it weighed only four ounces. It fits into your shirt or blouse pocket and costs only one-tenth the price of a cellular phone with just one-quarter the operating costs. Motorola is now manufacturing its Silverlink 2000 phone at the rate of 5,000 a week in Malaysia and selling it at the rate of 1,000 a week in Hong Kong and Singapore alone. Computer, fax, and satellite-delivered navigation signals will all be standard in any car built after 2001.

It is possible that future cars will run on air. One U.S. institute, Solar Energy Research of Golden, Colorado, is working on a process to convert atmospheric carbon dioxide (CO_2) into methanol for use in cars. Other companies, like Delco Electronics, are working on "self-driving cars" that would incorporate such features as obstacle detection, collision-avoidance, and radar-controlled steering.

Clothing will become even more diversified than during the 1980s and 1990s. Dress fabric interwoven with fiber-optic cables will light up or glow. A person's phone number might be included in a fabric's weft and warp so that it could be flashed to a desired partner yet remain barely visible to others in a crowd. Fabric that would appear loose and free-flowing could become tight and clinging upon command. This will be accomplished through a technique known as molecular shrinking in which an electrical current minimizes the area between molecules. The procedure is already used in some forms of metallic adjustable springs. Clothing designers will incorporate this and other advanced technologies into previously static fabric.

Life in the "crystal lane" (it will make the Industrial Age "fast lane" look like geriatric alley) will result in a rapid growth in monastic orders, based on the same tenets that caused them to dominate so much of Europe during the Middle Ages. Some people, feeling that the new age has too much change for them, will seek sanctuary from change in such temples of tranquillity. As in the Middle Ages, more men than women will follow that path. Women are more adaptable than men, and this will show up in their increased influence and affluence.

Research indicates that a sizable percentage of the population finds that receptivity to new types of foods and cooking processes increases adaptability to change. The world interchange of various ethnic groups, new cooking methods, and amazing new "crops" produced by biotechnology will accelerate this change. A food "explosion" during the late 1990s will appear even more astounding than the consumer electronics explosion of the 1980s. Most of these foods, as yet unknown because they haven't been invented (just as jet planes, television, computers, and satellites were not invented or even dreamed of in the early days of the Industrial Revolution), will be created by the new science of biotechnology. No doubt, some country will come out with "new people" as well.

This science will be so controversial during the years ahead that it will put the abortion issue on the rear burner. In 1989 the U.S. government approved genetic manipulation research on humans. Both the approval and the potential restrictions on it will have vast consequences for those countries that approve or disapprove of such practices. Biotechnology will basically mean the redesigning of the human body. Already, perhaps irretrievable steps have been taken that will result in our designing our own successors. Those who fight the process stand to lose incredible benefits. Those who support the process could unleash potentially hideous results. It will be the test of human intelligence to find a middle path.

By the year 2010 the planet will be "alive." The billions of human brain cells in each of us, connected via computer and fiber-optic cable, will be exchanging information at femtosecond speeds around the globe and at relatively inexpensive rates. This will accentuate the feeling of interconnectedness among all planetary dwellers. Some people, through such close electronic contact, will develop a sense of intimacy that could equate to a form of mental telepathy. Some younger children already report such feelings.

Photonics, the new science of acquiring, storing, and disseminating all types of media via light instead of electricity, will find a wide range of applications. It will make past advances, such as those in transportation, where we moved from covered wagons to jet planes, seem leisurely.

You can dread the future, or relish its challenges. The Chinese character for "chaos" also reads as "opportunity." The Chinese saying on luck and disaster presents another double meaning useful in describing the future: We live in interesting times.

→   ## Home Electronics

Almost everyone now has a VCR, but most people have never learned how to program it to record the desired shows. The new units make this much easier and can be programmed on screen. The latest models incorporate a "translator." They record shows simulcast in two languages. By pressing an extra button you hear one language and then another, or, if you want, both simultaneously. This is how the Japanese are now learning English.

TVs are everywhere today, but large screens will soon be a must to fit into your new home entertainment, information, and educational center. A vast number of channels is not far away. In 1991 we saw the introduction of Mattel's "Power Glove." Modified, this computer terminal on your wrist will allow viewers to use computers to handle shopping, banking, and stock market manipulations, and to select a sad, happy, or boring ending for favorite soap operas. It is also the first rustic tool with which you can enter virtual reality – the many new worlds within cyberspace.

To be current, you better build the cost of a good shortwave radio into your budget. They are no longer the crackly, static radios of the past. Today you punch in the digital frequency and get Cairo instantly. If you always wondered what those Morse code signals were saying, "Morse-a-Word" receivers will pick up the signal, translate it into English, and flash it along a reader board for you. Software programs that do the same thing on home computers are also available.

For your musical system, a stereo enhancer, equalizer, or real-time spectrum analyzer will give you enhanced sound. Either standard or cordless phones can be hooked up to your stereo system so you can really hear from your friends. This phone works anywhere in the world; you retain the same number for life; it weighs four ounces, and fits in a shirt or blouse pocket. The old-fashioned wired phone is on the way out because of the new craze for the "untethered" link of this second-generation cordless.

If you haven't yet purchased a CD player, go for the latest. The CD-ROM not only plays great digital sound but can deliver, for example, all the famous art works from the Louvre in Paris, the complete publications of NASA, the fifteen-billion-year history of the world, or the twenty-volume Grolier Encyclopedia – all on one side of the common 4.5-inch CD. It even handles disks for a Kodak Photo CD. Every home can now have a library on a disk.

What does the future hold? Expect Micro-TV for the home computer, which will give you the ability to select a single picture from TV, freeze it, and include it in a computer printout. If your electronic mail is discussing the eight new countries that entered the United Nations this month, include a picture of today's new map in that E-mail/fax to your mother.

Later on, expect full-time video on the computer screen, as compression transmission allows real-time video to be transmitted over present household copper phone cable. It will carry crunched information that expands once it hits a computer. The fiber-optic cable being hooked up these days will allow the contents of the U.S. Library of Congress, largest in the world with eighty million items, to be downloaded in thirty minutes.

Satellite dishes using the new 20/30, 60 and 90 gigahertz frequencies are now broadcasting in Japan. They carry the new High-Definition TV (HDTV) with 1125 lines of resolution that give crystal-clear pictures. Your present home TV shows 525 lines (when it's new and you're living next door to the transmitter). Present dish size is about that of a cafeteria serving tray. Other frequencies in the 60 and 90 gigahertz range, now in the test stage, will use a dish the size of a dinner plate and later still the size of a saucer.

Eventually, via holographic projectors similar to big-screen projectors, TV stars will come right out of the screen. They will be larger than life, to match the new prices, which will be higher than most of us can afford, at least for the first few years. Plan on watching your first holographic shows occasionally at the local pub.

→　　　*Hot Art*

Several years ago during an especially cold, wet fall day in Paris, I was pleased to notice as I sat at one of those delightful outdoor cafes that I was no longer cold, even though it was still raining on the umbrella over my table. That was my introduction to infrared heating, and I've been a fan ever since.

Now entrepreneur Gord Hamilton, who used to have a large, cold, and drafty house in Toronto (he now lives in British Columbia), has married art and infrared heating technology to produce a practical and inexpensive way to heat homes. Apartment owners who include heat in their rental charges should love him! He manufactures infrared heat panels with scenes painted on them. When framed, they look like works of art. But they are also low-consumption heaters that keep things warm – things like your body, your chair, and your table but not the surrounding air. If you don't heat that air you don't pay for it. The air can be several degrees cooler than your body, but you won't notice it because you are warm.

The cost is about one-third that of normal commercial heat such as oil, gas, or electrical baseboard heaters, and the "Cheater Heaters" come in three sizes. The largest uses 420 watts of electricity at a cost of about two cents an hour. The smallest costs about three-quarters of a cent an hour to operate. The "pictures" can be moved from one room to another – all that is needed is a 110-volt wall outlet. Budding artists can purchase the heater panel blank, apply their own artistic talents, and save a bit more on the pre-painted purchase price.

Some heating engineers still find this hard to believe, but Hamilton is producing these "fine paintings" on panels approved by the Canadian Standards Association, and they work. I purchased two to heat my office. Norm Elder, president of the Canadian Explorers Club, painted one with a jungle scene we experienced together during treks through the Kikori rain forest in Papua New Guinea. He thought it would be most appropriate for "hot art." Whenever I feel cold, I just turn on Norm's jungle scene.

→ *Heating with Paint*

Think of the money you spend heating your house, never mind what's spent on insulating material. You might want to consider painting your house with Rustol exothermic paint. The paint was developed in Japan and the company is bankrolled by Japanese yen. Just paint the walls. Electrical connections using either silver paste or copper mesh tape provide the hookup. Throw a switch or connect thermal sensors so that as you walk through each room you "turn on" your home.

The principle, although known to engineers for years, wasn't economic until 1990. Today the Rustol Corporation has produced a viscid exothermic paint. It is soluble in organic solvents and dries at room temperature. Its heating range is from 34 to 1,800°F. It requires only one hundred volts at ten amperes to create 1,500°F, although even twelve volts is sufficient for low temperature ranges. It does all this by allowing the electrical current to excite the molecules in the paint. That action creates infrared heat, costing about one-third as much as other electrical heating systems.

Because it is a viscid fluid, the paint can be applied to objects of any shape and a wide variety of substrates. It can be applied to metal, tile, slate, concrete, plasterboard, glass, and even heat-resistant plastics and fabrics. Think of the applications: plates, corrugated materials, pipes, molded products, and even toilet seats. Snow-melting is possible for roads, railways, and parking lots.

The company lists more than two hundred potential applications, from heating airplane flaps to pressing pants — even heated shoes and hair curlers! In one winter test project Rustol heated an eleven-thousand-square-foot car park for $7,400, compared to the conventional method costing $24,360.

Exothermic paint arose from Rustol's work on producing a heat-resistant anti-corrosion paint for use on automobile mufflers. After Rustol scientists succeeded in that task, they asked: If this paint is heat resistant, would it not be a perfect vehicle for a heat-producing substance? The result: MRX-001, with two types of electrical insulation, and a far-infrared radiation-emitting paint (MRX-002) enhancing heating efficiency. Next, they intend to couple MRX with solar energy.

In one demonstration Rustol engineers take a hotel glass ash tray, paint it, hook the painted ash tray up to their electrical source – and fry an egg in thirty seconds. Hot stuff!

→ *Outdoor*
Air-conditioning

A new technology called MicroCool offers air-conditioning – for outside. It takes air-conditioning where no human-made rapid temperature drop has gone before. In the process known as flash-evaporation, vaporized water molecules instantly evaporate causing rapid cooling in the surrounding area. It's not the mist that cools but the evaporation of the mist, a natural phenomenon.

A tiny nozzle with an outlet one-tenth the size of a human hair is the secret weapon in this war against heat. Ordinary tap or well water (very hard water may require additional treatment) is filtered down to five microns (one-twentieth the width of a human hair). The water is then pumped at up to eight hundred pounds per square inch by an industrial pump/motor combination. From this pump system, two manifold feed lines run to the desired area (typically a patio or swimming area) for cooling. Two lines of one-quarter inch atomizing tubes are installed along the entire patio overhang (and covered with a fascia board), with fogging nozzles every two feet, thereby enabling fogging zones to be established one foot apart. For areas with temperatures up to 100°F, only one line is required. For extremely hot temperatures, as in Saudi Arabia, an additional over-100°F line cuts in. Doors and windows can be left open; the cool air created on the patio may waft inside! Electrical and water costs are minimal at about twenty cents an hour. Mist evaporation cooling costs are reportedly lower than those for standard air-conditioning, although high winds and very high humidity can reduce efficiency.

After two years of testing in the desert country of the American southwest, MicroCool installations are now in auto service centers, retail outlets, hotels, and restaurants, including McDonald's and Burger King. One is reportedly in the home of a Saudi prince. More than five hundred installations have been completed in the Palm Springs, California, area in the past two years.

Not only humans are keeping cool: equestrian centers use the system to keep expensive horses and polo ponies in shape. Hothouse owners report that their plants now grow better. Agricultural installations from Napier, New Zealand, to Cheshunt, England, report improved growth factors with MicroCool. Some locations are now testing this system for growing plants aeroponically (without soil or water), and industrial sites are testing the process to make large indoor work sites more hospitable.

→   *Car Condos*

The new growth area for real estate? How about car condos. In Boston, car condos started selling in 1979 at the Brimmer Street Garage for a mere $7,500 each. Today, they fetch $130,000! In Brooklyn Park's Slope Garage, condos that sold in 1989 for $17,000 now go for $39,000. Down payments run from 25 to 40 percent with the balances amortized over ten to twenty years. Price depends on location. Sometimes buying is a bargain, even without considering appreciation, compared to renting a garage. In some other locations, the cost runs slightly more than rent.

This concept is coming from Southern California Edison Company, one of the largest electrical producers in America. Southern California Edison proposes a solar-powered carport with emission-free charging while the car is parked during the day. Conventional thinking about electrical cars has been that the main recharging would take place while cars were home in their suburban garages. The new thinking is that perhaps cars can be better charged, with less damage to the environment, when parked in an urban location, usually for six to eight hours. Now charging can take place at both locations. Suburbanites can charge supplementary battery packs during the day when the car is downtown, and this stored energy can then be used to top up a vehicle battery beside the house at night or when the weather has been overcast during the day.

With a few thousand electrically powered cars (and potentially 200,000 by the year 2000) starting to appear on the streets of California cities, Southern California Edison wants to be ready. Why? Because in a few years both car manufacturers and public utility companies will be obliged to produce a simple method to recharge electric vehicles. Once prices come down – and environmental taxes are added to gasoline-powered cars – the changeover could be dramatic. In a related project, Southern California Edison and the Los Angeles Department of Water and Power are cooperating to bring ten thousand electric vehicles to city streets by 1995.

This has created a partnership between Southern California Edison and the South Coast Air Quality Management District to produce a pollution-free recharging unit. The result: a carport with solar power. The roof of the three-thousand-square-foot solar carport would have photovoltaic solar panels to recharge the cars during the day. On rainy or dull days, power would be drawn from the regular power grid. Texas Instruments Inc. is working with the California utility to provide the panels. Although expensive at the moment, solar panel prices have been dropping over the last decade. When these three heavies get together on this project, breakthroughs may make solar power competitive with more conventional recharging alternatives.

If things work out as expected, Southern California Edison will have the first prototype fully functional within a year. Eventually they would construct car condos in public parking areas throughout their service area. "Park and Charge" will take on new meaning.

→   *Park without Coins*

How often have you parked your car, reached into your pocket and found no change? And when you leave your car to find some, you get that $20 parking ticket. So who's got a better idea? A Norwegian company called Park-O-Card. Their "social invention" can clear city streets of those inanimate highwaymen known as parking meters, downsize the bureaucracy, and provide municipalities with the same amount of revenue – at less expense. As a result, more money could go into general revenue to keep property taxes down.

Park-O-Card is a credit-card size device containing a microchip, a small long-lasting lithium battery, and a light crystal display (with a service life of fourteen thousand hours). Customers buy up to $300 worth of parking time from the city or parking lot operators. The cost of the card is absorbed into this initial purchase. You also now have a receipt for income tax purposes. Try getting that out of a meter!

Here's how it works: The card holder drives into a "zoned" lot that shows time and rates. You set your own built-in meter, and you attach the card to your sun visor, which you turn toward the driver's side window. The decimal point starts blinking to show that the card is working and also that you have a credit balance left on the card.

On returning to the car, you remove the card and stop its countdown, check for the amount left to spend on future parking, and drive away. No hassle. No money wasted on a pre-paid meter if you return early. And best of all, no parking ticket on the windshield.

This system eliminates parking meters. Saved are replacement or repair costs when the meters get hit by cars; high maintenance cost because of slugs, annoyed motorists, or the elements; and the cost of coin collection and possible embezzlement. Park-O-Card allows also more parking because, with painted street locations no longer necessary, small cars that take up less space allow more room for other cars. Park-O-Card can also be used for special-event parking.

This could rejuvenate city-core shopping. The card would work everywhere. Rates day or night and for differing locations could be adjusted by the city or lot owners with an on-location rate-card sign change, as conditions warrant. It's an idea whose time has come.

→ **The End
of Libraries**

In the age of the "knows" and "know-nots," the speed and cost at which data can be accessed is ever more important. A traditional library has to be accessed geographically. That takes time, a commodity of increasing value. And it usually costs money to travel to the library during its open hours, when your time may be more valuable elsewhere. You can't use less valuable time because libraries adhere to Industrial Age, non-user-friendly hours.

Consider the miniaturization trend in computer storage during the past two decades. In ten years we have moved from microfiche to computer disks. Single disks now are capable of holding more than an entire computer could hold just five years ago. Standard computer disks can now hold more than one megabyte on each side.

The computer world is being flooded with CD-ROMs, 4.5-inch plastic, aluminum-looking disks (the same size as the common musical CD) that can hold up to seven hundred megabytes of data – in multi-media. Each disk can hold one thousand 300-page books. What does this mean to libraries? One SERODS (Surface-Enhanced Raman Optical Data Storage) can hold the entire contents of the new public library in Vancouver.

Optical disk storage (and the sugar-cube-size crystals yet to come) will provide instant access, from anywhere in the world, for less than the cost of parking your car, to a Gutenberg-style library. Watch for even the dictionary description of the world "library" to change. We have all seen what widespread implementation of the low-cost fax machine has done for business and even the home. Wait until the library-on-a-disk moves in.

→ *Robots
at the Pumps*

It was only a matter of time. Now, in Danderyd, Sweden, near Stockholm, a company called Transrobot is manufacturing the gas station of the 1990s – a fully robotized operation. Drivers don't even have to get out of their cars.

You drive into a gas station, as in the old days, and park beside a Tankomatic box-pump, about three feet high. You insert a credit card into the terminal just outside the driver's window. Operating on high-precision sensors, the robot aims for a specially designed lockable adapter and cap, placed outside on all cars. The robot unlocks and opens the cap, inserts its nozzle, and the gas starts to flow. The nozzle is equipped with an airtight seal for vapor recovery. The driver watches the quantity of gas and progress of the operation on a terminal located near his window. If the car should move, or if anyone interferes with the equipment, the robot stops automatically. When it finishes filling the tank, the robot releases the car and locks the adapter. Then the driver retrieves the credit card and moves on.

Transrobot believes that its system should greatly speed up refueling at filling stations worldwide. A slightly more sophisticated system, which incorporates a fuel accounting program, has been designed for buses.

→ *Targeting
by Taste*

Until now grocery and other retail marketing has been based on saturation. The object: try to get everyone within your marketing area to shop at your store. Store owners today know what they sell but they don't know to whom. An upcoming generation of retail marketing systems will "lead retailers to an unprecedented dialogue with their customers," according to Thomas R. Newkirk, chairman of Direct Marketing Technology, Inc. (DMT), based in Illinois. DMT is a partner and developer with Retail Consumer Technology Inc. of a computerized database that tracks individual retail purchases. A store equipped with this system knows what customers prefer – it knows their tastes.

The system, called React, is described as a "reporting, response, and promotion package." React requires no special customer card to instigate tracking. Stores program cash registers to accept a telephone number volunteered by the customer at the time of purchase. Every transaction is recorded and matched to that number. The system, designed initially for retailers with a minimum of $7 million in sales, will shortly be supplemented by an update handling sales up to $70 million. Some thirteen hundred retail outlets belonging to The U.S. Shoe Corporation have been testing the program in conjunction with DMT. Six other chains are reportedly in negotiations for the system.

Customer phone numbers in the React system are processed by DMT through a reverse phone directory that matches the numbers with such demographic information as name, address, gender, age, income, dwelling type, and average purchasing power of the area. Most of this information is readily available from telephone white pages, city directories, or publicly available government statistical records. Purchases are recorded by product category or stock-keeping units. Method of payment is also recorded.

With this database, retailers know their customers better. They can make sure that merchandise the customers purchase frequently is always in stock. Retailers now have the same valuable information used by mail-order marketers. This leads to new cross-promotional possibilities. Marketing management now knows what customers are *not* buying. Retailers can conduct low-cost limited testing by drawing the attention of discriminating customers to new products before these go into mainstream sales. If customers cooperate further, anything is possible: reminders for birthdays and garden specials, and ordering of periodic large dog-food deliveries or floral surprises for certain dates.

Another food industry innovation may soon be the new inspector on the conveyor belt. Human inspectors become bored and sloppy. It looks as if their replacement will be a camera, two color monitors, and a computer that detects size and color abnormalities in potatoes, apples, and mushrooms. All photographs are digitized and assigned file numbers. Scrapes and cuts are easy to identify, but bruises are the big problem.

This development should reduce produce damage and spoilage considerably in years to come, especially when coupled with the now-under-development infrared ripeness beam and with the "artificial potato" that contains its own broadcasting system. The potato will, in effect, report on how it was handled from field harvesting to truck loading to processing plant!

→   Home Shopping
      for Groceries

Home grocery delivery is already a standard feature in most large cities, and more and more harried but well-paid workers are willing to pay for such services. Now that orders can be faxed from the office during coffee break, why not be the first on the block to have a twenty-first century "icebox," resembling a large rural mailbox, in the driveway? The food is there when you want it; you're not waiting until it arrives. The "icebox" is similar to a VCR, in that you set the schedule. Food is kept at the right temperature, with no puddle of melted ice cream reminiscent of the time you stopped to pick up the dry cleaning and got trapped in a traffic jam.

Such an outdoor refrigerator would lock after being loaded by the grocery delivery person. Coded credit cards would open it when you arrive home. A spouse might even have your favorite drink, complete with ice cubes, waiting for you in the driveway fridge when you step out of the car.

Some working couples waste as much food as they eat. Frequent delivery of smaller quantities would reduce waste, though do nothing for the cost factor. Convenience compensates for increased cost. This concept could result in a change in food retailing as great as that introduced by the twenty-four-hour convenience store.

The nature of food will change, too. Researchers at the U.S. Department of Agriculture, for example, realizing that smaller units of food will be in demand by smaller families, have created a tiny lettuce that should be on the market by 1995. It will be as tasty and as crisp as full-size lettuce and, with delivery to your driveway fridge, it won't have a chance to go limp in the sun. Perfect for small families who can't eat a whole head of lettuce while it's still fresh and for restaurants that get calls for single-serving salads.

Remember the "reach out and touch someone" ads of the phone companies? Before the turn of the century you will see the "reach out and touch that food product" version of virtual reality move into the home. Picture this: You're out of food. It's raining, the streets are slippery, and your car has been acting up. What to do? Turn on the TV, dial in your favorite supermarket, and take a video stroll down the aisle (with music to shop by). You first put on a virtual reality glove, then reach through your TV screen to that shelf with jars of genetically adjusted "jungle health beans" from Costa Rica, the latest rage. Naturally you can turn the jar around first to read the health-affecting contents shown on the label.

Shopping in this manner gives you an "electronic shopping cart" you don't even have to push. It automatically records items purchased and their cost. To return anything before you reach the checkout counter, hit the cancel button on the screen, and the item will disappear from the cart and the tape. Electronic taste and smell stimulators won't appear for a few more years, until new-style sensors are available. But they too are coming.

→ *Video Carts*

Information is power. Now Information Resources Inc. of Chicago and others plan to "entertain and extract" information about your lifestyle and shopping preferences by using "video carts," while you stroll up and down the aisles of your favorite supermarket. Imagine a flat six-by-eight-inch video screen on every shopping cart handle. Sometimes the screen will show a map of the store, offer recipes, and ask questions. Developers say that ads will constitute 15 percent of the video programming, and the remainder will be an in-store video "newsmagazine."

Why would grocery stores want this? Because grocery researchers know that two-thirds of all food-shopping decisions are made in the store. Not you? Check your shopping lists. Most lists have a maximum of ten items, yet most people hit the checkout counter with more than thirty items in the cart. How does that happen? Researchers know, and they believe they can profit from your shopping practices.

The system is high-tech. First, the commercial comes in via satellite from Information Resources Inc. to each store's computer. From there it's broadcast by in-store radio waves to each cart. But it doesn't show up yet on the cart's video screen. Why? Because the customer isn't close enough to the shelf on which that product appears. When the customer gets close to that shelf, an electric trigger plays the ad on that cart only. When the customer checks out, the electronic cash register tells store management how well the idea is working.

In-store advertising, now a $12 billion business, will grow at an annual rate of 17 percent, according to the trade organization Point-of-Purchase Advertising Institute (POPAI). In a relative sense such advertising is inexpensive – about one-third that of prime-time network TV spots.

Another company, Advanced Promotion Technologies (APT), has already started handing out coupons at checkout counters after shoppers have been introduced to in-store interactive video screens and printers – to reward shoppers for their interest! APT then determines how many people have purchased the items covered by the coupons by monitoring the checkout counter. APT has booked test arrangements with Ralston Purina, Kraft, Del Monte, and Procter & Gamble (who own a slice of APT). Another company has commercials spreading the word on shoppers' car radios as they drive into supermarket parking lots. And the Atlantic & Pacific Tea Company is testing ads and special listings on electronic signs in some of its stores as you read this book.

→   *Talking Posters*

You're walking along a subway platform one evening waiting for the next train. An election poster on the wall shows the smiling face and white teeth of a political candidate. As you pass, the poster speaks. "Remember to vote next Tuesday." You stop and study this poster, which would normally be lost in the maze of poster ads. You're hooked. It's another Japanese innovation: talking posters or "transmittal art" to its supporters.

Two examples of talking posters recently exposed to the public in Japan were a young lady, in an election publication from Nagoya, and a group photo telling citizens how they can participate to create the new city-concept for Shizuoka. The operation is fairly simple and the same speaking-mechanism chip can be reprogrammed for a different poster. The framed poster can be easily hung or relocated. But it must be hung securely to prevent souvenir seekers from pinching it.

For the first time conversation has become visible. As a display piece for show rooms, exhibition of new products, sales campaigns, and service counters, talking posters may be the forerunner of other such media. Triggered by an infrared sensor and adjustable to a range of between three and fifteen feet (it works in total darkness), the talking poster unit runs on AC or DC power. It can operate for two months on six 1.5-volt batteries. It is available in playback times of eight, sixteen, twenty-four, and thirty-two seconds and is prevented from continually talking by a ten-second delay between "speeches." Recordings will not fade for a year even with a power failure. More than 300 60-second replays can be performed in one day.

Posters range in size from about ten by twelve inches to thirty by forty inches. They come complete with transparency film and a panel board and frame equipped with an AC power connector.

As an information news service, a guide at counters or festival sites, or as a bulletin board and talking guide directing people to leisure or other facilities, this is the newest way to go. Expect rock concerts, movie spectaculars, and election polling booths to start using the "talking posters" in the near future.

→   *Airborne Advances*

How often during long flights have you looked forward to the movie only to find that you've already seen it? Why can't airplanes have multiscreen theaters, allowing you to select from three, six, or even ten movies?

Now you can – at least on some British Airways routes. Each seat has a small television screen in its back, connected to a video selection control that lets passengers take their choice of six TV channels. This is a first for the fare-paying passenger in the European skies (although not the first ever; some private jets and a few Middle East aircraft have had something similar). These screens for individual viewing are part of the first-class enhanced service on British Airways.

The high resolution, three-inch liquid crystal screens are designed for an aircraft's varying light levels. The system allows a passenger to select from six different productions, including sports, music, news, popular TV shows, feature films, and children's programs. Sound is delivered through electronic headsets, so nearby passengers are not disturbed. Shows rotate approximately every four hours depending on flight duration. A total change in the show packages occurs every month. This new inflight entertainment in British Airways aircraft is called Airvision and is a co-production of Philips Electronics and Warner Bros.

A similar version has been patented by Sony in Europe. This system works like satellite television in apartment buildings. A bank of receivers (VCRs in the aircraft) play different movies. A cable, under the floor of the aircraft, carries all the signals and is designed to "leak" weak FM signals throughout the aircraft. Built into each seat, along with the individual TV, is an antenna that picks up the signals and carries them to the screen. You choose the show you want. This way a wide selection of shows is constantly available to all. You watch when you want to and not when the flight attendants decide you should. The same set can carry stereo sound and video games, and you can even operate both simultaneously.

It doesn't stop there. Sony says the same system could incorporate a word processor, a floppy disk drive, and a printer. Passengers could work on corporate reports or compose letters. As they left the plane, they would receive a floppy disk containing their data, or a paper printout if they had so instructed the seat-back computer. Coming next? Transmission of such data via modem or fax from the plane while en route.

5

Medicine and Biotechnology

→   *Brain Scans*

We know more about outer space through the use of optical and radio telescopes and recent space flights than we do about a mysterious terrain closer to home: the human brain. This land has its own mountains and valleys and mysterious interior, locations as exotic and forbidding to the new age explorer as a remote planet.

Although it makes up but 2 percent of our body weight, the brain consumes 20 percent of our energy. This strange electrochemical world provides the power to think. And thanks to recent technological developments, we can now in many ways see *where* we think. By means of an expensive assortment of technologies called a cyclotron, scientists have produced radioactive isotopes. (Isotopes are atoms of the same element that have different mass numbers.) When injected into a human vein, radioactive isotopes allow another modern medical technological miracle – the Positron Emission Tomography

(PET) scanner – to see what is happening inside the brain as it happens.

Long a believer in direct experience, I became part of a control group to explore this most important territory. It couldn't have been accomplished without the help of Dr. Donald Calne, of the division of neurology at the University of British Columbia's Health Sciences Research Centre, and Dr. Brian Pate, director of the PET program. Their usual scans are conducted to assess and analyze damage done by such diseases as Parkinson's and Alzheimer's.

First I received a slow injection of the radioactive isotope fluorodopa. It takes about twenty minutes for the radioactive material to collect in the brain cells. Outwardly, the subject should appear and feel normal. Inside, the lights are changing, but only the computer can see them. The procedure itself is painless, almost boring.

The PET scanner looks like an expensive, oversize, horizontal hair dryer. Similar to a radio telescope that "sees" the stars, the PET scanner has the power to see what is optically invisible. In this manner it differs from the Computed Axial Tomography (CAT) scanner, which is in most major hospitals today, or from the Magnetic Resonance Imaging (MRI) scanner. The CAT sees if the shell is cracked; MRI checks the white and gray matter. Both of these see inside the cranium but cannot discern if the brain is actually functioning. They see the territory but cannot determine if there is actually life there.

The brain is "sliced" electronically and the resulting picture appears on the various video monitors. In my case, these monitors were located both in the room that contained the PET scanner and in an adjoining room where other research staff were controlling the computer and monitoring the results. Brain activity shows up as colored or illuminated areas. This is made possible by the brain's use of the body's glucose, which has been made radioactive.

Medical staff can now compare healthy brains with diseased or damaged brains. They can see what is happening inside the head without resorting to surgery. Surgery may be the only recourse for a person who is brain-injured, but now doctors have a clearer path to get to the damaged portion. The PET scanner also paints a clearer picture of brains damaged by disease.

X rays were a big advance, enabling us to see into the fleshier portions of our anatomy. Now we can literally see ourselves thinking. As we come to understand more fully exactly *what* we are seeing through the PET scanner, the implications will be tremendous.

→   *The Gamma Knife*

We have learned more about the human brain during the past decade than in all previous history. First, the CAT scanner revealed details of the cranium. The MRI scanner showed us the gray and white sections of the brain. Then the PET scanner revealed the electronic activity in the brain. Quantified Signal Imaging (QSI) moved us onto new ground, adapting an older technique, the Electroencephalogram (EEG), to produce a map of our thinking processes.

Now the gamma knife performs neurological surgery without the scapel. Credit for developing the first prototype twelve years ago in Sweden goes to Borje Larsson of the Gustaf Werner Institute at the University of Uppsala and to Lars Leksell at the Karolinska Institute in Stockholm. The gamma knife showed that a directed energy source could be an effective treatment for brain tumors. The Presbyterian-University Hospital in Pittsburgh is home to this latest bit of medical-science technology. The only two other units outside Sweden are in Buenos Aires, Argentina, and Sheffield, England.

This unit converts cobalt-60 in a new technique called stereotactic radio surgery. In effect, it sends an electronic knife into the brain to dissolve dangerous tumors. Length of treatment can be as short as fifteen or twenty minutes. Most treatments do not require general anesthesia and cause no immediate side effects.

The gamma knife, which has met the exacting standards of the

U.S. Nuclear Regulatory Commission, is safer than many existing procedures. It eliminates risky, open-skull operations. Television monitoring is used during the procedure and two-way voice contact between the physician and patient is maintained at all times. Patients usually leave the hospital the day after the operation.

Because more than fifteen hundred patients have already received treatment at the Karolinska Institute with no deaths, the gamma knife is not considered experimental. Of five hundred patients at the Karolinska Institute who were suffering from arteriovenous malformations (AVM), 87 percent had their AVM completely obliterated by this treatment. Another 11 percent had theirs partially altered. Tumor growth was prevented in 90 percent of other cases. A wide range of brain problems can now be treated with this procedure.

At the Presbyterian-University Hospital, the patient's head is placed within a large helmet-like device. The attending physician adjusts the radiation through small openings called collimator ports. This allows a great deal of energy to be directed to the intended target inside the brain. Every ten years or so a robot reloads the unit with the radioactive cobalt-60 material.

→   *Low Vision
     Correction*

More than ten million Americans and one million Canadians have visual defects that cannot be corrected medically, surgically, or with glasses. Approximately 25 percent of this group have a form of impairment called low vision. In the United States there are about 2.5 million people with this problem. Now comes new hope: a form of "intimate TV" in the shape of wraparound glasses that carry their own TV camera.

Specialists at the Johns Hopkins Wilmer Eye Institute and at NASA will employ space technology to develop a device designed to improve low vision. The first phases of the project are expected to run for at least five years. Arnall Patz, professor of ophthalmology and director of the Wilmer Eye Institute, says, "As soon as it is perfected, the final version of the enhancement system will be distributed widely to eye institutions throughout this country." It is anticipated that rights to the device will be licensed to a Canadian company shortly thereafter.

The enhancement will not restore lost sight but will help patients make best use of their remaining vision. The system is expected to benefit patients with central vision loss, the part of the vision normally used for reading. When the device is worn, the patient will see the world on two miniature color television screens where the lenses of eyeglasses are usually located. Lenses and imaging glass fibers will be embedded on each side of the wraparound section. The lens will form images of the scene in front of the patient on the surface of the fibers. These fibers, similar to those used to carry long-distance telephone signals, carry pictures back to miniature solid-state television cameras carried in a belt or shoulder pack. These images will be processed by a small battery-powered computer system in the pack and then displayed on the television screens. Development of this product centers on how images must be altered and enhanced for the person with low vision. The designers say the device will be lightweight and comfortable. And the glasses won't be odd-looking. Young people might even find them "cool": The outside of the television screens will appear similar to the mirrored lenses in some sunglasses.

→ *Eyes, Teeth –*
What Next?

A few years ago I had a plastic lens surgically implanted in my right eye, which had the very poor vision rating of 20/300. My vision improved almost instantly to 20/30 and within a few months to 20/18. I began seeing better with one eye than I ever had with two eyes and glasses. A year later my ophthalmologist performed the same operation on my left eye with similar results. Within months, vision was 20/20 and has improved since then. My driver's license was renewed without the "corrective lens required" restriction. The federal Ministry of Transport (MOT) renewed my helicopter and my land and sea aircraft pilot's licenses, and I passed the necessary flight test with an approved MOT check pilot.

Thanks to medical expertise and a piece of plastic about the size of a pinhead, I went from white cane to control column. The eye operations seemed simple: each had taken thirty minutes and was less trouble than having teeth cleaned by a hygienist. They were less troublesome than a root canal.

After this successful personal test of current high-tech ophthalmologic medicine, I looked around to ask, "What's next?" The answer: surgically implanted titanium dental "pilings." The pilings implant went like this. After a full mouth and jaw inspection, the dental surgeon gave me a wraparound X ray, similar to having your jawbone structure photographed by a panoramic camera. With that information in hand, the surgeon, the dentist, and a nursing assistant proceeded to slit an area of the gum vacated by two lower left molars years ago. They drilled two vertical holes into the jawbone, inserted two titanium pilings covered with protein, screwed them into place, put plastic covers on the top, and stitched up the gum. There was some pain the first evening, but none after that. The gum was sensitive for a few days. The slight swelling disappeared after ninety-six hours. A week after the operation, the stitches were removed.

I was instructed to return in four months to have the gum slit open again, piling covers removed, and new ceramic teeth screwed into the tops of the titanium posts. In the interim, the protein covering the titanium pilings would trick the bone into thinking the titanium implants were another part of the jawbone and would build up natural bone around them, giving complete structural support to the new teeth. They were better in some ways than regular molars. In the X ray of the completed project, it looked like two large nails had been driven into my jawbone, a picture reminiscent of the cranium operations of early Aztecs that I had seen in *National Geographic.*

Why did I try this new procedure? I'm in my seventies. The dentist said it would minimize teeth trouble and save the remaining rear molar. I would also have a balanced set of lower teeth and could continue to eat well for a few more years. Most dental surgeons limit the operation to the lower jaw, as the bone structure there is stronger and more extensive.

Today more than three million body implants of various kinds have been conducted in North America and the success rate has been surprisingly high – about 80 percent in teeth implants and from 70 to 90 percent in many other implant operations that are now almost standard.

Then came the bad news. I fell into the 20 percent failure category. My body rejected the implants. I'm too healthy: My immune system would not tolerate the intrusion. The surgeon slit the gum, removed the titanium pilings, and stitched me back up. The gum healed within a week.

Now, let me see. What could I try next . . .

→ *Positive*
   Identification

Since James Watson and Francis Crick first conceived of the DNA helix as a microscopic spiral staircase, we have learned more about our physical structure at the molecular level than in all past history. Governments in the United States, Japan, Europe, and elsewhere are rushing to interpret the human genome, those strands of life that identify all the genes in the human body. That is a big project. There are more than ten trillion cells in the human body. They all contain DNA, which tells us how we grow, look, and sometimes die.

No two people, except identical twins, have exactly the same DNA pattern. Positive identification is relatively easy. The smallest sample of blood, hair, skin, or bodily fluid can distinguish us from everyone else on earth. I now carry a holographic representation of my DNA (deoxyribonucleic acid) code. Any part of me is recognizable forever in the hologram. My DNA code was provided by Lifebank, the world's first private DNA identity storage center.

The implications are many. For example, there need be no future "unknown soldiers." Anyone can be identified, from the smallest shred of bodily tissue available for forensic scientists. Disaster victims can be identified if any body part has been located. Original samples remain the property of the people they were drawn from (or their next of kin).

Working with physicians and hospitals, Lifebank arranges for a collection of a DNA sample from your baby at the moment of birth. Blood samples can be taken from older children and adults at a doctor's office. Using state-of-the-art techniques, the sample processed through DNA profiling is identified and stored at Lifebank. The owner of the DNA report receives a "passport" with the registered DNA identification number, which allows immediate identification.

Acting solely as a repository for such DNA codes, Lifebank conducts no tests and maintains no extensive data files. It provides parents with the knowledge that, at any time in the future, they can identify their child – under any circumstances. Samples are coded to guarantee confidentiality and are deposited, under tight security, in a storage facility where they are protected against extended power interruptions or natural disasters.

Unlike more traditional methods of identification, DNA profiling is virtually 100 percent accurate. Although there is controversy over the procedure in some quarters, it has already been accepted in more than a hundred trials across North America. A report from a congressional study released in August 1990 said that DNA fingerprinting is "reliable and valid" enough to be accepted as evidence in criminal trials. The writers of the report from the Office of Technology Assessment also called for technical standards to insure that all laboratories can produce the same results.

It certainly beats the heel-printing practice at maternity hospitals. Poor prints, identity bracelets, and fingerprints all have demonstrated shortcomings. "Fingerprints can be changed, for instance," says Lifebank research scientist Dr. Christine Dietzel. "They can be changed with plastic surgery. Heel prints can be smudged. Bracelets can be lost or switched. DNA can never be altered. It's inherent to the individual."

→ *The*
Mosquito-eater

In most of Canada and the United States, mosquitoes are an accepted nuisance. As one who has had malaria in Cuba and dengue fever in Haiti, I can attest to the serious problems mosquitoes present in semitropical and tropical areas. Although my hallucinations during dengue fever were colorful and wonderful, the more serious diseases such as yellow fever and encephalitis carried by these insects can be deadly. There has been no proof yet that mosquitoes can transmit the HIV virus, but even that possibility cannot be ruled out.

A simple new device may help reduce the incidence of mosquito-borne diseases. It may be the world's most effective mosquito exterminator. A small suction fan draws insects into range with an ultraviolet light lure, and when they reach a fine mesh "killing field," a self-cleaning, spinning nylon thread acts as a garrote. Called the "Dynamic Flying Insect Exterminator" (DYNEX), the device was conceived and developed by James Woodruff of the Pacific International Center for High Technology Research (PICHTER) in Honolulu. The prototype unit contains a small model fan about eighteen inches in diameter, but the unit could easily be built up to nine feet across for outdoor use.

Unlike previous insect exterminators, DYNEX simplifies removal and recycling of expired insects. After being killed and diced by the whirling nylon, dead insects drop into a small drawer at the bottom of the "cage." Accumulated insects can be used as fertilizer or food for birds and fish. DYNEX creates no startling noises as high voltage zappers do. The unit handles bugs of varying sizes but does not affect honeybees and butterflies. The ultraviolet bulb is easily replaced. It's really three appliances in one, as it also serves as a light and an air circulation fan.

The unit contains built-in safety features. The spinning thread will not harm the hands of children or adults. The mosquito-eater is environmentally friendly. No pesticides are used and the Science Congress says the unit is virtually silent and can be used indoors and out. The simple design also lends itself to inexpensive manufacture.

→   *Biocomputers*

Biocomputers will change the face of medicine before the start of the third millennium. Scientists have now sucessfully bonded a human neural brain cell, grown in tissue culture, to a Motorola 68000 microprocessor. This is the first step in a process that will allow direct interconnections between humans and the inorganic. The implications are clear: humans are no longer evolving along an exclusively organic carbon-dated path. I can see the day when children will be bionic from birth.

These new discoveries are occurring at the Playfair Research Unit of the Toronto Western Hospital. This team of medical researchers includes Dr. William Tatton, vice-president of research at Toronto Western and founding director of the Playfair Neuroscience Unit, and Dr. John K. Stevens, professor of biomedical engineering at Playfair. Their three-dimensional imaging techniques modeling the human nervous system are said to be one *billion* times more sophisticated than any other circuitry. They are trying to incorporate these techniques into a system that may be the answer to spiraling medical costs.

By the late 1990s biocomputers will have mapped the human

nervous system, which appears to be by far the most sophisticated communications system yet found. Eventually we will be able to send specific messages via human dendrites to specific cells when instructed. These internal body communications will tell the body to accept implants, for instance, thus "turning off" the body's normal rejection system in this particular area. They could also instruct the body to release more (or less) of certain body chemicals to correct imbalances or specific diseases. Messages can be directed to a specific site or a specific disease.

Just as industries have realized that they must spend more on research and development if they are to stay in business, so too some hospitals are arriving at the same conclusion. Without solutions to the rising cost of health care we might find outselves burdened with hospitals financially unable to operate (no pun intended).

The research is being directed to reduce the economic burden of ill health. Many brain disorders hit people when they are young, destroying their productive years. These patients then require other people to spend their lives caring for them. The cost over the years is tremendous. Almost any breakthrough releases millions of dollars for other, yet unsolved problems.

The first goal is to build a sixth generation supercomputer capable of changing three-dimensional geometry to silicon-based circuits that simulate brain circuits. A further goal is to produce biochips, where the cell and the chip come together. Then will come the use of living membrane processes to replace the silicon interface. This is all part of the new emerging field of bioware. It is showing that the human nervous system is a similar but much more complex system than any microcomputer network. The complexity of what Playfair is attempting is shown by the fact that ten million or more eye cells handle more computing in one second than the present model of Cray Supercomputer could simulate in one hundred years.

The long-term results? One day we will be able to program our body to fight illness, disease, and physical injury. It is revolutionary – and evolutionary!

→   *Biotechnology
and Religion*

For the past 2000 years, especially in the Christian world and increasingly in the Middle East, religion has made an indelible impact on the human race. In Asia today there are stirrings of a new immaculate incarnation that is spiritually free of any sexual connotation: robot religion. Like the European cathedrals of the Middle Ages, new monuments of worship are materializing. The new head office of the Bank of Asia in Bangkok is built in his/her/its image – a robot.

Our view of religion is about to change because of technology. The oft-repeated phrase "only God can make a tree" is no longer true. With the mastery of genetic manipulation, humans will start designing their successors. With this will come increased diversity. Some may want artificial gills for living in the sea. Some may want to fly like birds. Impossible? A man in the Gossamer Albatross flew across the English Channel on mere muscle power.

Totally new subspecies will be created, eventually appearing as aliens to other new subspecies. Many will be bionic. In prehistoric times, our human ancestors climbed down from the trees. Some climbed back and stayed there. Others stood upright and took a different route, and we are the result. Another fork now beckons along the evolutionary road. Some will try to stay where they are, as some simian ancestors did in the past. Others, many others, will take the new fork in the road. We don't know where it will lead, but it will be different.

Researchers in Indiana and Nevada have succeeded in transplanting bone marrow from adult humans into the embryo of a sheep. What does this mean? At one year old, the test sheep was producing both sheep and human blood cells. This is another major step in the field of biotechnology, in which certain genes can be transferred from humans, animals, birds, reptiles, insects, and even certain plant species into other organisms.

Researchers are using gene transfers to aid in the prevention of fatal or disabling genetic disorders. Sheep in Scotland have for some time been producing Factor VII and Factor VIII, the blood-clotting component that prevents people with hemophilia from bleeding to death from small wounds.

What will development in biotechnology do to our morals, our philosophy of life, our sexual habits, our creativity, and the economic dominance of certain cultures? We do not know – but the impact will be severe, shocking, impressive, and delightful. The growing shortage of diversity in living things will be replaced by an overabundance of new species, some made by biohackers – bright young kids using equipment currently available on hardware, supermarket, and drugstore shelves. The world will never be the same.

The mechanical world removed us from farming in the country to working in cities, doubled our longevity, and gave us homes that were warm and dry. The biotech world will change things in ways we can no more dream of than yesterday's illiterate farmers could have imagined the cities, computers, airports, or luxury hotels of today.

We do know that biotechnology will continue to be one of the major fields of technological development in the 1990s. The U.S. government has approved the registration of patents on new life-forms, even though under an older piece of legislation, the Anti-slavery Act, humans could not be owned. If they were now cloned, that concept might not fit under the old legislation. It hasn't been tested in court – not yet.

One form of clone, a "medical" mouse, has already been patented. Other patent registrations have been applied for and are now being processed. In many ways it is irrelevant whether the United States or any other major power approves of new life-forms. The reality of today's world is that if the United States doesn't, some other country will. The potential economic advantages inherent in such developments will prove irresistible.

Cyborgs, clones, chimeras, and other life-form mixtures will arrive whole, or in part, before the third millennium. Will we be able to accept this massive change in philosophy, religious outlook, and technology? Countries that can accomplish and handle such change will rapidly advance. As for countries that can't – remember the Luddites?

→   *The Cyborgs*
      Among Us

In the Agricultural Age muscles and stamina provided a living. The Industrial Age demanded some muscle along with some intelligence. But the Communications Age can forgo the muscle. It demands brainpower. Some people will become stronger intellectually when they can do things with information that the majority, at least for the moment, are unable to access or process. Enter the cyborgs.

There are more than two million cyborgs in North America today. Every day they go about their business in all parts of the continent. Their appearance and performance probably give no hints about why they are different. But they are cyborgs – living organisms who have had one or more vital facilities replaced by pieces of technology. From people with nylon hip joints to those with prosthetic appendages or surgically implanted eye lenses, like mine, they are part of a growing and in some ways superior segment of *Homo sapiens*.

Until recently, people became cyborgs only because of accident, age, ailments, or other disabilities. An even more subtle movement is taking place. We are designing our own successors. No one in centuries past has ever experienced the accelerating change of the past decade. We are creating a new species.

Recently I filed patent registration applications for CyberSight, an application of intra-ocular implants that goes even further than the bionic lenses in my eyes. Imagine a television/computer screen containing an ocean scene of someone snorkeling. From that computer runs a thin fiber-optic cable, smaller in diameter than a human hair. It is plugged into the eyebrow of a young woman. She is able to see, in another room or building, or even overseas, the picture appearing on that computer/TV screen. She is a cyborg with electronic-assist.

She is receiving assistance similar to that felt when you first drove a car with hydraulic steering. New knowledge can be fed directly to her implanted intraocular lens by cable or radio waves. The plug-in model is a small medical "snap-fastener" implanted along with a transducer or radio receiver. Either can be implanted separately.

Consider this scenario. A firefighter enters a burning warehouse. (Even insurance companies recognize the danger; firefighters pay a much higher insurance premium than police officers.) He sees and feels the heat. Fortunately, this firefighter is a cyborg. He radios the fire department command car to bring up the blueprint of this warehouse and the list of contents – those are now part of the Geographical Data Interface (GDI) being created by progressive municipalities. That data appears as an overlay on the reality background of his normal vision. The cyborg notes that explosive and toxic materials are in one corner of the warehouse and calls for increased water power to be applied to that quadrant of the blaze. Other fire crew immediately start to remove or isolate such material. Building sensors may be sending information about conditions in areas not yet covered by other firefighters. The cyborg will check on these from signals he receives directly from the sensors. This cyborg-firefighter gets much higher pay than the rest of the crew. No one minds. They know his superior ability is saving their lives.

Or this scenario. An undercover police officer is lounging on a street corner in a seedy end of town. Just down the street, he notices a character he dimly remembers. Through his body-pack radio he calls police headquarters and gets switched to records. "What was the name of that guy who drowned those three people in a swimming pool in Surrey two years ago?" "Boyd, Harold Boyd," replies Records. "Send me the mug shot." It flashes on his internal eye screen while he casually looks around. "It's him. Send back-up fast. I'm on the southwest corner of 9th and Alder."

The ability to see what others do not would, of course, be of tremendous advantage in many segments of global business. If computer transmissions could be sent, as they are today, via radio waves not only to your PowerBook or other laptop but directly to an implanted receiver, so that the transmission appeared as an overlay or double exposure on your current vision, the possibilities in cross-cultural training, say, or underwater archeology, would be amazing.

Consider the possibility of a video camera that could take pictures similar to X rays. The video camera could transmit images at the speed of light to someone with CyberSight who would see immediately what the X-ray pictures looked like – no matter where he or she was!

We now have sophisticated home barometers or "weather stations" that indicate slight variations in barometric pressure, temperature, and humidity. Such sensors, highly miniaturized and implanted in humans, could provide an early indication of a hurricane or earthquake. Wrapped in a tiny plastic package, almost any sensor could be implanted with a high chance of success.

Infrared food machines have already been developed for testing degree of ripeness and spoilage. Next, sensors implanted into cyborg fingers could instantly determine, with a high degree of accuracy, the stage of a particular fruit or vegetable at the moment. The savings in spoilage could be monumental.

Your fingers could also contain sensors to measure pulse, blood pressure, heartbeat, menstrual cycle, chemical imbalance, toxic blood, and perhaps even manic-depressive stages, schizophrenia, and brain tumors. Such detection devices exist today. Tomorrow they will be shrunk in size to be implanted in people. Such people would be more capable than most nurses or even doctors in many circumstances. The pay scale for such superhumans should match their abilities, convincing many to have such implants.

Farfetched? Most future scenarios are, the first time you hear them.

→   *Plant Diversity*

The world is awash with purveyors of doom and gloom, pointing out that species of some sort are disappearing every few minutes. The doomsayers leave the rest of the population suspended in horror with the image of a shrinking world. A decreasing diversity of crop seeds, for example, is predicted to lead to a monocultural corn or bean that someday will be the victim of a new disease, and we will all starve in an age of pestilence and famine.

Exactly the opposite is more likely to happen. Consider crop diversity. With conventional thinking, a lost species of plant or animal was gone forever. Although we should of course not deliberately eradicate any species nor encourage obvious polluting or environmentally dangerous actions, look at what is happening as laboratories and research centers around the world are experimenting with creation. Genetic manipulation has already accomplished feats impossible in the past. The abilities of one species, both animal and plant, have already been transferred not only into another species of the same family but across species lines. In what may be called the breakthrough of the age, the gene that causes the glow in a firefly has been transferred to a plant. There are now tobacco plants that glow in the dark.

We may be losing plant and animal species now, but we will not be losing diversity in the future. Indeed, the question will be what to do with the over-abundance of diversity. Within this decade, supermarkets will provide not only foods you never tasted before but foods that didn't exist before. And if this seems far out, remember that some extinct species may be resurrected via DNA revitalization.

Today's fantasy is tomorrow's reality. The science in *Jurassic Park* may be questionable today, but the notion behind it will one day seem as ho-hum as the thought of a man on the moon.

→   *Human Antifreeze?*

Two hundred years ago, if you had suggested that virulent diseases could be eliminated with injections of a modified version of the disease itself, the Western world would have considered you a practitioner of witchcraft. Yet in 1798 Dr. Edward Jenner proved that his vaccine could prevent smallpox. Today that dreaded disease has been virtually eliminated. Other vaccines have markedly reduced the incidence of cholera, typhoid, tetanus, diphtheria, polio, influenza, and rubella. Vaccine therapy works on the principle of stimulating the inherent healing powers of the body to conquer infection by increasing available antibodies to attack invading bacteria or viruses.

Since you don't get drowned today for practicing witchcraft, I am going to suggest that someday an injection will be developed to prevent or delay the human body from freezing in the cold. And once injected, the body will be protected for life. Here is why I can be so bold. Among the fish that can stay year-round in the cold waters of the North Atlantic are two unique species: ocean pout and winter flounder. These fish can stay in water that is below freezing, although such cold is a sure killer for all other fish. Even the hardy Atlantic salmon moves out when temperatures approach the freezing level. Scientists studying the winter flounder have discovered that this dowdy flatfish has within its dull body an antifreeze protein that lowers its blood's freezing temperature by retarding the growth of ice-crystals.

With gene manipulation now being practiced in laboratories around the world, it is just a matter of time until that thermal gene will be transferrable to many other organisms. New trails are being blazed in Memorial University's Marine Sciences Research Laboratory in St. John's, Newfoundland, where scientist Arnie Sutterlin is working to make such a development a reality for local hard-pressed fishermen. He wants to make Atlantic salmon able to survive and thrive in icy Newfoundland winter waters, just as the winter flounder can.

According to fish physiologist Garth Fletcher of the same institution, the flounder's liver is responsible for this biological magic. So the answer was simple: find the antifreeze gene. Thanks to the wonders of biotechnology, the project is well under way. The gene has been implanted in Atlantic salmon eggs. Now not only are scientists trying to make salmon grow larger, more rapidly, at lower cost, but they also want them to grow where they have never grown before – in freezing water. Such gene-manipulated eggs would hatch into salmon that would have the antifreeze gene in every body cell.

Malaysian-born Choy Hew, a fellow scientist in Newfoundland, had been working on flounder protein structure involved with the then-unknown antifreeze gene in 1981. He learned that scientist Peter Davis of Queen's University in Kingston, Ontario, had also successfully isolated the first of the flounder's forty antifreeze genes. The total package started to come together. Later, an intestinal bacterium known as *E. coli* was injected with the flounder's alien gene. Generations of nonunion bacteria, working twenty-four hours a day, produced millions of copies of the desired gene.

Today Fletcher and his colleagues believe that 10 percent of his gene-manipulated salmon have "taken" the gene. If the gene can be transferred naturally as they reproduce, a new, more sophisticated salmon will ply the North Atlantic. This has not yet been proved, but the process has come a long way in a relatively short time. Nature might have taken a billion years to isolate and transfer the antifreeze by accident.

Biologist Kenneth B. Storey of Carleton University in Ottawa has recently found another animal – the painted turtle – that regularly freezes in winter and thaws out in the spring with no harmful results.

It appears that the turtle knows how to dehydrate by removing from its cells the freezing water that would normally puncture and fatally damage blood cells. When warm weather returns, the shrunken cells absorb the thawing water and revive.

Storey believes that someday this knowledge may make it possible to refrigerate human transplant organs for weeks or months. He does not believe it will be possible to freeze a whole human body because of the complexity involved. But then twenty years ago, he couldn't have imagined what he is doing now.

6

Food and Farming

→ *Boutique Farming*

In North America the family farm has been shrinking for two hundred years. Now the possibility of a renaissance is on the horizon. A new development may increase the number of small farms. With such naturally occurring plants as potatoes, eggplant, celery, corn, and cabbages, anyone who buys the seed can grow and sell the plants. Not so with patented plants developed through biotechnological methods. These plants are protected under patent regulations and may only be grown by private arrangement with the patent holder.

One possibility is that small "boutique" farmers may in future operate similar to owners of McDonald's franchises. They will enter into a contract with the patent holder to handle the "product," the way a car dealer handles Honda or BMW. The boutique farmer will purchase the seed; plant, grow, and market the product; and agree to participate in broad advertising campaigns supported by all growers tied in with this product, which is what happens with a

McDonald's franchisee. In return the farmer will have the right to be the only grower of that product in a given area – perhaps as few as five or ten farmers per state or province.

The real innovation lies in a product developed by manipulating genes into a new plant. It might look like a carrot, but it might be green or red, and it might also offer relief from a particular allergy. The technique of transferring genes from one plant to another is already well established. Imagine the implications of transferring a gene from the insect, animal, or human world across the gene barrier into the plant world. Theoretically, any gene from any living organism can be moved into another living thing. As mentioned, researchers have succeeded in transferring the gene that causes the glow in a firefly into tobacco plants. And the University of Guelph Agricultural Department has hatched chickens – with the heads of quails!

Along with the possibilities of unusual, nutritional, and perhaps medically potent foods produced in this manner, new methods of growing such products will develop. Many fruits and vegetables will be grown inside, year round, and in vertical rows. Plants can be grown in what appears to be a large, vertical sewer pipe with open "windows" encircling the pipe at regular intervals. The patented seed is planted within these windows and grows out through the openings to reach super-pure sunlight collected on the roof of the "farm" by a device, similar to a satellite dish, that tracks the sun. Fresnel lenses collect and intensify the sunlight and feed it down to the plant through fiber-optic cables. On the way down, a process called a "light shift" removes the infrared band of light, which is redirected to help warm the building. The harmful ultraviolet portion of the light spectrum, which burns tomatoes and people, is discarded; only pure sunlight reaches the plants, allowing them to carry out photosynthesis. Solar panels on the roof collect additional sunlight and turn it into electricity. This is stored until the hours of darkness to provide the additional light required to bring a total of twenty-two hours of "sunshine" each day to each plant.

Irrigation of the plants requires far less water than on flat, open land where much of the water evaporates or runs off. The same applies to fertilizer that runs off in heavy storms or filters through to the water table when the plants do not take in the quantity applied to the soil. The vertical drip system ensures that each plant receives precisely the moisture and fertilizer it requires.

There are other advantages. These farms can operate year round and thus can contract with hotels, restaurants, and grocery stores to provide a known product every day of the year at standardized prices through the seasons. With this type of operation, a ten-hectare indoor farm should be able to produce the equivalent of what is now grown during five or six months on a 400-hectare farm.

→   *Micro-propagation*

During the next decade there will be more changes in food production than during the past millennium – all thanks to biotechnology. One day we may be able to produce vegetables, fruits, flavors, fragrances, drugs, and some industrial chemicals independently of the plants that we now depend on.

In San Carlos, a town on the fringe of California's Silicon Valley, the Escagenetics Corporation is testing various ways to develop the flesh of oranges and cherries without growing the trees. It will do this in vitro: growing the fruit in giant fermentation flasks in an environment that will change the meaning of "hot house" forever. The company is also working on date- and oil palm tissue. This is one of a series of projects based on micro-propagation – growing tree fruit in vat cultures.

Escagenetics now has United States and overseas patents on its phyto-vanilla process, which it developed by growing a cell culture in polymer beads in a flask in the laboratory. This is not an artificial vanilla flavor. It is identical to the true vanilla flavor. Almost 100 percent of true vanilla comes from the vanilla bean orchids of Madagascar, an island in the Indian Ocean off the African coast.

Obviously, such developments pose social and economic problems for such Third World countries that have depended on one-crop economies for centuries.

The mundane and lowly potato, the fourth major food crop in the world and a staple in North America and elsewhere, is another example of how biotechnology can make a difference. The method used for centuries in potato planting is expensive and time-consuming. It takes about one ton of tubers, used as the "seed," to plant one acre. With the new "true potato seed" (TPS), that same acre can be planted with only five ounces of TPS! Think of the savings in storage and transportation costs. The seeds are virtually disease-free and are less costly to produce than seed potatoes. They could be planted with an air gun.

Such seeds are protected by a coating against bacteriological infection and insect, rodent, and bird depredation. Escagenetics has developed "elite parent" potatoes, many derived from subspecies that originated in the Andean region of South America and in Mexico. These, when crossed in certain combinations, produce vigorous high-yielding hybrids. The company says that from the tests now under way, it will be able to produce more than a million plants within a year through micro-propagation. These potatoes will be uniform in texture, flavor, and color, with improved culinary characteristics.

TPS is now planted in Egypt. Egyptian farmers apparently don't feel right about planting the very small potato seed, nor do they have the required equipment. So Escagenetics plants its own seeds in an extremely dense pattern on a seventy-three-acre farm in that country. When the seeds have grown to the size of a golf ball, they are dug up and sold to Egyptian farmers who apparently have no objections to planting these mini-tubers that look like potatoes. Planted in early February, the potatoes are harvested in early summer.

Escagenetics is also testing its developments in Turkey, Spain, and Pakistan. It is learning to operate globally, while many in this field try to push the sale of traditional products. The moral? Learn to change as the world changes.

→ *Aeroponics*

During the early days of the Industrial Age, the big investment opportunities were in mechanical inventions and the modern production lines of automotive and other factories. Today many big opportunities lie in the biological "factory." One fast-moving field has been the perfecting of hydroponic methods of raising food (growing plants in nutrient solutions without soil). While this has created some amazing results with tomatoes, lettuce, cucumbers, and other vegetables, it hasn't yet become consistently profitable.

Now an advanced form of that technique – aeroponics – may produce much of our food in the future. Aeroponic plants are grown in air; their roots are not covered by soil or nutrient solutions. New possibilities for producing food this way are emerging from research into methods of feeding those who may one day live in outer space. The Experimental Prototype Community of Tomorrow (EPCOT) center, a part of the twenty-seven-thousand-acre Disney World near Orlando, Florida, is growing crops in this way. Long conveyors carry the plants around the Kraft Foods "Creative House." During part of the cycle, plant roots pass through a spray box and receive a shower of water and nutrients suitable for that stage of growth. In another technique, lettuce is grown on large A-frames; the roots are sprayed from the inside with hydroponic/aeroponic solutions.

This is similar to a process I observed in 1985 in Tsukuba, Japan. There, during a six-month period, fifteen thousand tomatoes grew from one seed! The plants grew fifteen feet high and thirty feet across, and the seeds were not even genetically altered. Researchers had similar success with cucumbers (seven hundred from one seed) and musk melons. They were growing lettuce in just four days – practically while you wait! And it was all done inside, in the shade.

Another emerging technology with vast implications is the marriage of computers and genetic engineering. Crops such as strawberries, pineapples, bananas, and sweet potatoes are asexually propagated clones. They are not grown from seeds. Using tissue culture, and a technique that regenerates whole plants from tiny pieces of leaf or even single cells, staff at "The Land" pavilion at EPCOT dissect leaves under a microscope. They place these tiny pieces in a vitamin-laden hydroponic solution, along with sugar and hormones. Thousands of tiny new plantlets quickly spring from this rich nutrient solution. Along the way scientists are incorporating new characteristics into various tissue cultures to improve plant growth; for example, to provide plants with a tolerance of drought and salt and a resistance to pests.

In meat production, attempts to eliminate diseases and pests in cattle, such as the parasitic larva of the heel fly, are being tackled in a new fashion. The heel fly larva causes a loss of hundreds of millions of dollars each year in meat and hide damage in North America. If this can be prevented or even minimized, retail meat costs might be affected. Hoechst Celanese Corp. and the Codon Corp. of San Francisco are working together to develop a vaccine against such cattle grubs. They will attempt to isolate and clone the gene for an immunogenic protein. Again we have a development that uses methods unknown just a few years ago.

At one time 98 percent of the population of North America were farmers. Today farmers make up only 2 percent in the United States and 3 percent in Canada, yet we produce more food than our present North American population of 275 million can eat. The farm of the future will be a highly scientific operation with computers and robots. This has already started to happen – and the implications will be revolutionary.

Five thousand years ago, an Egyptian farmer had the technology to work a one-acre plot and was able to feed five people. Four thousand years later in England, a farmer could work five acres, but feed only three people. By 1875, with the new horse-drawn machinery, an American farmer plowed 140 acres, feeding his family and six other people. In 1986 the average American farmer worked 435 acres and fed fifty people. The total value of machinery required to do that, for all American farmers, was $111 billion. The trend continues – larger farms, more capital investment.

Far too often the interest burden from borrowed capital cripples farmers and forces them into bankruptcy. Yet the future will be even more capital-intensive. Tomorrow the costs will appear astronomical, but the results will match the costs.

And what of the implications for farmland? For years we have been hearing dire tales of farmland lost to housing and commercial development. In several countries innovations suggest that the farmland we are spending so much energy to protect may be the last place to grow food in the future. In light of this potential global change, are we being realistic?

In Japan, the Ajinomoto Corporation has produced genetically constructed bacteria that excrete cellulose, the basic component of our forests. Ajinomoto is producing an elastic paper so fine that Sony is already incorporating it into diaphragms for top-of-the-line acoustic headphones. Another potential use for the same product is as artificial skin for burn patients. This production is taking place in a "factory" – no farmland involved. Since fine paper can be produced to such demanding tolerances, perhaps eventually newsprint will be produced from waste.

Mitsui Industries has moved in on the flower industry. Mitsui has produced virus-free lily bulbs, which previously required a large field, in an antiseptic vat the size of a desk. The Kirin Brewery Company spends just under $100 million each year on research. Roughly 80 percent goes into biotechnology research, mainly on vegetables. Last year Mitsubishi Kasei spent almost $150 million on research, half on such products as genetically improved rice. Meanwhile, Kyowa Hakko Kogyo Co. is researching a new approach to wine-making that may be setting a trend for the future. It fused three strains of yeast and produced a rosé called Fusion Bio, a much purer bouquet. No vineyards were required because the grapes are grown in vats.

Agricultural changes are happening faster, over a wider global area, and involving more products, than ever before. This trend can only accelerate. Think of what this could mean to the value of farmland. And think of the political implications for governments locked into a fixed agricultural policy.

→   *Farming in Space*

The space program has yielded many benefits, the most obvious being communications and remote sensing satellites. The satellite "parking lot," located at an altitude of 22,300 miles over the equator, contains the geostationary satellites that bring the world the nightly news and carry a high percentage of overseas telephone calls. Remote sensing satellites in other orbits are already used extensively in assessing crop potential, disease, plant condition, soil types, water content, insect infestations, and plant stress. Other benefits of the space program are appearing in ceramics, high heat-resistant auto parts, houses, cutlery, robotics, and sensing equipment. Now some of the early work in "space farming" is beginning to look promising.

Dr. Thomas Heppenheimer, an aerospace engineer on the NASA scientific team, suggests that farming in space may be a major benefit of the program. Under the rigid requirements of space, productivity means survival (as it is coming to mean on earth). Dr. Heppenheimer and his colleagues believe that ten thousand people in space could be adequately fed on a mere 151 acres. The reason? Crop yields would be ten times greater than on earth because of the twenty-four-hour-a-day sunlight, continuous year-round growing season, and exact control of water, plant nutrition, temperature, and carbon dioxide for each type of growing organism. All this without such harmful things as storms, hail, drought, frost, rodents, weeds, pests, and diseases, which reduce food production. Such crops as corn could be forty times more productive than on earth.

What may prove even more beneficial is what we have learned from research on food for use in space: that there are more than eighty thousand edible plants in the world, and that worldwide we are eating less than three thousand (or 4 percent) of them. The big three – wheat, rice, and corn – together provide half our protein and calories. Twenty-four other cereals supply another 45 percent.

What the potato and the tomato did for the dietary habits of Europeans three hundred years ago will be duplicated and expanded during the late 1990s and the early years of the third millennium as we learn how to use, grow, and distribute widely some of these other seventy-seven thousand edible plants.

→   *A Better
     Apple Tree*

Growing fruit on trees involves some problems: the space necessary for human movement between wide-spreading limbs, the difficulty of reaching fruit on higher branches, and the fact that the fruit doesn't ripen simultaneously. A development now under way in Britain and using an apple tree native to British Columbia may solve some of those problems. What might it mean to produce handlers and consumers? Lower prices, because of more efficient harvesting techniques; better fruit; and a distinctly different look to apple orchards of the future.

The East Malling Research Station, a branch of Britain's Institute of Horticultural Research, is attempting to grow apple trees to resemble flag poles. The advantage? Trees grow closer together – less than a yard between trees and between rows – allowing for greater use of robotic pickers, which results in considerable savings at harvest time. The flagpole tree also permits more trees per orchard, producing higher returns per acreage.

The species of apple selected for these experiments is the wijcik, a sort of McIntosh from British Columbia, which grows like a sturdy natural cordon. This species grows limbs more like spurs than normal branches, so the flowers and fruit are borne up the single main stem. Scientists found that when the wijcik was crossed with varieties of other apple trees, half the resulting seedlings were more compact and columnar – a result of the dominant gene in the wijcik species.

Other features crossed into the wijcik have improved fruit and tree qualities for various horticultural uses; for example, producing easy-to-manage trees for amateur growers and trees that flower at the same time as more conventional orchards, thus acting as space-saving pollinators. Distribution of the new seedlings is probably taking place this year. Test stands have been under way at several assessment centers in Britain since 1986. Municipalities might also someday be planting these trees as compact ornamental highway dividers. Their red flowers, brightly colored fruit, and purple or cut-leaf foliage are highly decorative and would brighten up roadways.

Of course, kids will have more trouble climbing these trees than the apple trees of our youth. Biotechnology, like hard technology, causes unpredictable social change!

→ *Livestock*
Reproduction

In 1945 North American dairy farmers, with twenty-five million cows, were producing almost all the milk the market required. Today they fill the increased demand with just ten million cows. How do they do it? The "scrub" cow has been turned into a milk factory by improving the breed at a rate far faster than nature could. The technique that makes this possible is artificial insemination, which has been in widespread use for the past thirty-five years. Today 70 percent of those ten million dairy cattle in North America become pregnant through artificial insemination. The bulk of U.S. turkeys are bred through artificial insemination, because – according to Dr. George Seidel of Colorado State University, an authority in this relatively new field – breast meat is now such a large portion of male turkeys that they cannot "get close enough to females to mate reliably."

Another popular technique is embryo transfer. The first reported successful embryo transfer involved a horse in Japan in 1974. This nonsurgical method had a 40 percent success rate when first introduced. Today surgically implanted embryos in cows have reached much higher success rates – up to 72 percent. In this method a high-quality cow is inseminated and a week later technicians recover up to six embryos by irrigating the cow's uterus. These are then placed in surrogate "scrub" cows, which carry the high-quality calves to birth. Dr. Seidel points out that "commercial use of embryo transfer began about fifteen years ago, and today 100,000 calves are produced annually by this means in the United States and Canada."

This is just the beginning. These animal reproduction technologies have moved ahead so fast that the slower, older methods have already been bypassed. Scientists create "new" animals and plants by gene manipulation inside an embryo using the technique of "transgenesis." If an animal or a plant has a desired gene that prevents disease, improves lactic flow, or produces a "jungle pharmaceutical," this gene can be inserted into the "new" animal or plant. The resulting improved trait would then carry on in all the offspring of that animal. Various existing systems, such as gene injection, retrovirus delivery, or incorporating desired genes into undifferentiated embryonic cells, make this relatively simple. A newer technique is the transplantation of cellular nuclei. According to Dr. Seidel, this could yield thousands of identical offspring.

Even more exotic techniques are gynogenesis, birth by female parents, and androgenesis, the production of offspring by two males. "Researchers have already bred poultry, fish, and amphibians from parents of the same sex," says Dr. Seidel, "although not for commercial purposes." Tomorrow will bring animals that never existed before. Animals will not only carry genes from other species but will also deliver offspring that come but from these female/female and male/male parents. There will be cloned animals and plants in the thousands.

And they will be superior animals, more quickly reaching higher levels of breeding and production than those achieved during past decades by artificial insemination. They will be stronger physically and will produce better products for the food market. Because of their increased value, they will be treated like expensive thorough-bred horses. Environmental sensitivity is automatically built in to this increased productivity. Obviously ten million cows consume less food and produce less methane gas and run-off effluent than twenty-five million. Besides helping to keep food prices low and quality high, this puts fewer demands on the environment.

Admittedly, the ethics in patenting such animals are being questioned. But patenting or trademarking has been going on in plants for decades. Roses are a common example. Dr. Seidel comments that "the economic benefits for consumers will be significant. Buyers will see a greater variety of food and fewer food-borne diseases. Even more important, the improved animals will produce larger supplies of food, which will lower prices, since demand for food is relatively inelastic." During the past decade the price of beef, in constant dollars, has dropped by almost 50 percent, and milk in the United States also costs less.

Farmers who do not keep up with such developments will be unable to compete. Farming will be based increasingly on information and intelligence and will be a far higher (and better paid) calling than in the past. If all this sounds dramatic, remember that the improvement process has been going on for centuries. Farmers have always tried to breed better strains. Now biotechnology has set up a moving sidewalk to handle the quickening pace of genetic change. If we don't use these new technologies here, we won't be competitive. You can bet they will soon be used elsewhere.

→ *Improving*
the Tomato

Scientists at Cornell University in Ithaca, New York, have done considerable work on the tomato. While researching a relatively unknown Brazilian tomato known as Alcobaca, they found that it contains three times as many desirable biochemicals as an ordinary tomato, which allow it to remain firm and fresh much longer.

Almost all market tomatoes grown today are picked while still green; otherwise they would perish before reaching the grocery shelf. Because farms aren't next door anymore, growers, shippers, and grocery stores have been forced by commercial considerations to transport green tomatoes. The Alcobaca must mature to ripeness fully on the vine, and vine-ripened tomatoes are always tastier. The Brazilian development will enable supermarkets to stock ripe tomatoes for ten to twelve days, extending the current shelf life of four or five days.

The Cornell scientists are also researching other chemicals that may work along with the ingredient known as 1,4 butanediamine, found in the Alcobaca tomato. They are looking for the "shelf-life gene." If they find it, food deterioration may become a thing of the past. Impossible, you say? Right now the United States, Canada, and other countries are working together to decipher the entire human genome or genetic blueprint. Similar work in a plant genome program would tell us how some plants handle pests, drought, high heat, or other stresses. When we discover the plant that does it best and has the ideal gene for the problem, that gene could be transferred to other plants to give them the desired feature. The net result will be superior plants and superior food.

There are also medical applications. Common barley plants may be the biotech "factories" of the future, producing medical compounds at a minute fraction of today's costs. Interferon, insulin, and tissue plasminogen activators are all believed to be suitable for this new technique. At the moment, pounds of animal tissue must be processed to gather a single ounce of interferon. This lengthy process is very, very costly.

Now the breakthrough: ordinary barley seeds are being turned into superseeds that will manufacture such valuable pharmaceutical proteins by the pound! Researchers remove from the seed the genes responsible for the enzyme alpha-amylase. Properly triggered, barley normally can produce large quantities of this substance. But now scientists substitute genes that code for a desired protein. Such "fixed" seeds are then grown into seedlings and plants like ordinary barley. But at harvest time, the superseeds are removed and germinated. They do not grow like their forebears; instead they produce huge quantities of the desired protein. One acre of barley could produce in just three days enough seeds to produce twenty pounds of a particular protein. The process hasn't yet been perfected, but it's just a matter of time.

→   *Foods with*
           a Future

Twenty-five years ago, in the heyday described in John Steinbeck's *Cannery Row,* the harbor at Monterey, California, was producing up to 250,000 tons of sardines a year. During the early 1970s, the catch dropped precipitously to just sixty tons. By 1978 Cannery Row was a ghost town. Today it is the home of the renowned Monterey Bay Aquarium – built mainly through the generosity of David Packard of Hewlett-Packard computer fame who donated more than $50 million toward its construction. The aquarium has been a catalyst for an upsurge in tourism on the Monterey peninsula, but another economic catastrophe is taking place. This time the food is abalone.

Landings in California of wild abalone of all species have been dropping steadily from a high of 2.8 million pounds in 1961 to about 300,000 pounds by 1985. The latest figures show further reductions in recent years. With any product that grows scarcer, the price rises. Where once a top price of $4 a pound was big news, today's market commands nearly $30 a pound.

Unlike the sardine industry of Cannery Row, however, the abalone industry has a future. Abalone Resources Inc. of Vancouver is now using intensive aquaculture with the aim of eventually exceeding the natural catches of the past. The company's research and management team has been using technologically advanced systems to produce – on land – abalone eggs in huge quantities at their facility at Morro Bay, California, south of Monterey.

Abalone Resources, the largest such facility in North America, now has more than 1.25 million red abalone growing in size from less than a quarter of an inch to more than 1.25 inches. A new "grow out" facility is planned for the mid-California coast west of Guadalupe but the project was not without problems. Clearing environmental regulation hurdles took three years and considerable funding. The pilot plant will be expanding into full-scale production. And who'll buy all this abalone? If North Americans don't want it, the Japanese do. Last year they bought six million pounds of abalone from Australia, New Zealand, and Mexico.

Meanwhile, the Japanese are growing a mushroom the size of a hamburger and it tastes like steak. By creating a unique environment with controlled temperatures and watering techniques developed especially for growing this mushroom, the Japanese company Kabushikikaisha Akita Inc. is opening up a new market. According to spokesman Masanao Kubo of Asahi Foods, the company in charge of production in Japan, the mushroom spores are cultured for between forty and forty-five days until they reach full growth. At the precise time that they peak in flavor, aroma, and texture, they are picked. They can then be thrown on the barbecue, providing an instant, low-cholesterol, low-fat "meaty" delight. Such mushroom "steaks" have most of the vitamins and minerals contained in beef but far less protein. They will be available in Tokyo restaurants this fall. The company will also be providing the technological know-how for overseas production to provide fresher mushrooms and low transportation costs.

The reaction from the cattle industry is predictable enough. Janet Williams of the Beef Industry Council says, "For those people who don't have beef available, it [the mushroom] may be of interest, but I would be surprised if it would be a significant product in the United

States." Sound like the reaction of the U.S. auto industry in the late 1970s when Japanese autos started to enter the country?

→ *High-Tech*
  Snack Food

Even snack food is going high tech with biotechnology. One eager aspirant in the field is DNA Plant Technology Corp. of Cinnaminson, New Jersey. Food researchers there claim that their first generation of "vegisnax" will be crispier, crunchier, and sweeter than "ordinary" vegetables. They will also be more nutritious with a lower calorie content. This will be the newest in fresh, ready-to-eat vegetables in snack-size packaging. Consumer test panels gave high marks to their original test products and now a second generation of these lines is being developed with even more desirable traits optimally combined.

You will hear more in future about the value-added plant-based products now being developed for both consumer and industrial markets. Basically, the desirable characteristics in a wide range of vegetables, cereal grains, tropical plants, and other crops are being greatly enhanced through variations of clonal and protoplast fusion techniques. Thanks to biotechnology, these characteristics can be made to appear in such crops in a much shorter time than they would with traditional breeding techniques.

Desired traits include increased solid content for processing tomatoes; superior-tasting fresh tomatoes; and crispier, crunchier, and sweeter carrots, celery, and other vegetables. Enhanced flavors and fragrance compounds that naturally occur in various plants are being introduced genetically into other plants. And the oil, starch, and/or protein content in corn, wheat, and rice is being enhanced genetically.

In a joint venture with Koppers Company, DNA Plant Technology is also working on a disease diagnostic kit to detect turf grass diseases. With Campbell Soup Company it has a joint venture to develop improved varieties of processing tomatoes (a $500-million annual market) and fresh market tomatoes (another $500-million annual business). It is also in partnership with Firmenich of Geneva, Switzerland – one of the major world players in the flavor and fragrance field – to use biotechnology to develop new, cost-effective, reliable methods for manufacturing various plant-derived raw materials for this industry. A half-dozen other major companies have also turned research contracts over to DNA Plant Technology.

→   *Edible Holography*

"Edible holography" is the newest marketing ploy to hit the confectionery counter. The applications are endless. Holography will eventually appear on cookies, cakes, cereals, seasonal chocolates, and child-oriented candies. Hungry entrepreneurs will find a zillion other uses for this innovative idea as soon as the first products hit the marketplace.

Holograms, which you may have seen on magazines, credit cards, and record albums, are about to appear on grocery shelves. The holograms are produced by molding a layer of imperceptible microscopic ridges directly onto a product and incorporating the regular ingredients of the product itself. Light striking these tiny – one or two microns in depth – surface ridges is diffracted, creating vivid colors and shapes, which appear to move and float within the food itself.

The process fits in with modern tastes. It uses no dyes, pigments, chemicals, or other additives. Color is not added but is extracted from the visible portion of the electromagnetic spectrum and appears in or over your cake or other product using the technique developed by Dimensional Foods Corp. The technology creates the color from a physical rather than a chemical basis. The same technique allows animation and realistic three-dimensional illusions without affecting the product in any other way. According to Eric Begleiter, founder of Dimensional Foods and a "food imaging inventor" (there's a new occupation), holographing a product does not affect the taste, texture, or "mouthfeel" of the product. Begleiter thinks that "this process could become a widespread replacement for other methods of food coloring and decoration."

It's Mother's Day and your mother is a chocaholic. Why not combine a Black Forest cake with roses? The chocolate surface of the cake will be molded with the microscopic ridges mentioned and presto: when the light is right, a bouquet of roses appears to be hovering just over the cake! Imagine Valentine's Day, the Fourth of July, Halloween, Christmas, and birthdays.

Another process allows colors and images to be encapsulated inside transparent materials. Think of the day you tell your kids they're going to Disneyland and confirm it with lollipops bearing Mickey's logo – and he moves when held up to the light. One product being developed is "Rainbow Sparkles" – granulated particles with brilliant highlights that sparkle like diamonds in all the hues of the rainbow. When applied to the surface of foods, the Rainbow Sparkles are invisible, but they cause the food to sparkle in the light. Candy coins that flick from heads to tails are also possible with this process. Talk about virtual reality. Holograms change the color of the product and appear three-dimensional. It gives new meaning to the phrase "playing with your food."

Dimensional Foods is also developing methods for embossing compressed tablets with holographic colors and images. These images would represent a new means of differentiating brand-name products from those of competitors. It could also be a method to prevent product tampering, as any break in the hologram would be vividly apparent.

Dimensional Foods does not manufacture products itself. Its business is licensing this technology for appropriate applications. The North American confection market is in the $8 billion range; cookies are a $3.5 billion business; and the pharmaceutical market is worth $25 billion. Dimensional has obtained a broad, pioneering patent covering ingredients, manufacturing processes, and products used or created in connection with its technology.

→ *Robot Harvesters*

In the not-too-distant future, the oranges you eat may be untouched by human hands. Robotic orange pickers now being tested at several locations around the world can analyze a fruit for ripeness by color, determine its location on the tree, and zoom in for the picking. "Robots could revolutionize the harvesting of oranges and other fruits," says Roy C. Harrell, professor at the University of Florida's Institute of Food and Agricultural Sciences.

Many methods of picking oranges have been tried in the past. Some researchers tried to blow them off with jets of air. Others tried tree "shakers" coupled with catcher's gloves or frames. None really did the trick. Now, programmed with super senses, the technically efficient robotic picker will be commercially viable within a few years.

The prototype picker with its camera-equipped picking arm is mounted on a mobile control vehicle. Improved models might have many arms, operating simultaneously and transmitting feedback information to be stored in the robot's computer memory. Automatic recall could remind the robot of oranges, originally green on the first pass, that should now be ripe for picking.

Sonar units, such as those on automatic focus cameras, measure the distance from the orange to the picker and direct the arm to the target. In one model, a rotating lip goes behind the fruit, clips the stem, and lets the fruit drop into the waiting receptacle. The entire operation is completed in seconds, allowing a rapid sweep through rows of ripe fruit. According to Harrell, a multi-armed unit would be able to harvest six oranges per second! The only human involvement would be a single person to position the unit at the start of the row of trees. The same technology could be suitable for apples, peaches, and other fruits.

This particular technology was developed after publicity attracted the attention of an Italian equipment manufacturer, who gave a research grant of $204,000 to the school. The prototype picker, after one final field test in Florida, was shipped to Sicily.

→ *Agnes the Sow*

If you still think robots are confined to the factory floor, meet Agnes, the robotic sow. From a prototype developed at the University of Guelph in Ontario by animal psychologist Dr. Frank Hurnik, Agnes was upgraded to commercial production by Farmatic Inc., a Canadian specialty farm equipment company that is changing the whole concept of farm production. Agnes promises to be the greatest development in pork since laser cutting and blast freezing. This robot will go a long way to reducing production costs, minimizing early litter loss, and producing a healthier product. Bacon and ham sales may eventually increase because of lower retail prices.

Agnes has some advantages over nature's model. It's no secret that young piglets have a tough life. Many litters have mortality rates of between 15 and 25 percent. There are various causes. Sows roll over and crush or smother piglets. Almost every litter has a runt who gets pushed out of the feeding line. Often the litter is larger than the number of nipples the sow has available. Sometimes the milk runs out. When that happens, all the piglets could die. Another factor is post-partum separation; after delivery, some sows refuse to feed the litter, or resort to outright killing of piglets.

Agnes has a much pleasanter temperament. Picture this idyllic scene from the robotic-sow-equipped farm: piglets sunning themselves under infrared heat lamps are summoned by "mother" Agnes with a "dinner call" grunt. The light over their resting deck goes out, and the light over the nursing robot, simulating the sow's body warmth, lights up. One minute after dinner call, milk formula containing all the proper ingredients for that stage of life flows by gravity from a refrigerated unit (holding a twenty-four-hour supply) located in the feeding pen. En route the milk passes through a thermal bath that warms it to 102.6°F. Immediately another faster-paced feeding grunt signals food is available. Up to sixteen nipples are available, so no one gets left out. Extra space between nipples prevents crowding. Every piglet in the litter obtains the required nourishment. At the end of two busy minutes, the nipples shut off and flush automatically. The nursing light fades as the resting deck light comes back on. The piglets scurry to the new heat source and fall asleep until the hourly feeding cycle is renewed. Other litters can be fed during the intervening fifty-five minutes. Mixture and volume is adjusted from half an ounce for newborns to 1.75 ounces for three-week-old piglets.

Agnes is non-union, performs twenty-four hours a day, needs no rest, eating breaks, or holidays, and can handle several litters simultaneously. She adjusts food, medicine, or growth stimulant content automatically based on the piglets' growth stage, and has a robust body that resists abuse. She also leaves no mess to shovel.

The unit operates on a twelve-volt system and incorporates miniature heat pumps developed by NASA for cooling satellites. They are only one inch square and perform both heating and cooling functions. Grunting sounds are digitally encoded on a microchip and programmed into the cycle by a microprocessor. Piglets raised by Agnes are reported to have better dispositions. Some animal psychologists believe this is because robot-reared piglets never have to compete for milk. Blair Gordon, Farmatic marketing manager, says the only thing the company hasn't incorporated into the units so far is an appropriate sow aroma.

→   *The EnviroCaster*

For millennia farmers around the world have planted according to the seasons. Until recently they had no method of precisely predicting the prime time to plant. Weather predictions could only be vague, and even the most accurate forecasts have never applied to a particular farmer's exact acreage. Every farm, big or small, has its own particular environment. What's good for one on Monday may not be suitable for another until Wednesday.

EnviroCaster is a self-contained, computer-driven environmental monitoring instrument that spends twenty-four hours, seven days a week, measuring, recording, analyzing, and remembering all the environmental factors – good or bad – that affect a farmer's crops. The unit can tell when apple scab will hit your orchard (not the neighbor's), when downy mildew endangers your onions, or when coddling moths are starting to emerge. No more guessing. It's all based on the fact that scientists know what combination of weather conditions are likely to "turn on" plant diseases or trigger insect infestations. Complex formulas, until recently used only with main-frame computers, are now available through EnviroCaster to forecast high-risk periods.

Plants, like people, are subject to stress. Frost, scorching heat, high winds, and lack of water all exact their toll. The EnviroCaster provides accurate records of frost, temperature, solar intensity, wind velocity, and rainfall on a particular acreage. Using this instrument, you know the best time to fertilize or spray – not only to improve crops but also to minimize damage to the environment. The same unit with appropriate software handles turf farms, golf courses, and other large lawn areas.

EnviroCaster can precisely monitor air temperature, degree days (from four different dates and eleven base temperatures), dew point, leaf wetness, rainfall, relative humidity, soil temperature (at two depths or locations), solar intensity, wind direction, and average wind speeds. If the farmer is away, the record for the past fourteen days awaits his return. Units come with rechargeable batteries and a solar-powered charger, built-in printer, degree-day accumulators, assorted sensors, daily weather history memory, downloading ports to other computers, and assorted cabling.

Sound like the end of the *Farmer's Almanac?*

7

Communications

→ *The Information
War*

Ten years ago a brash sailor named Ted Turner from Atlanta took a
bankrupt television station and turned it into the money-making
Turner Broadcasting System (TBS). It includes the Cable News
Network and Headline News (CNN), the TBS Movie Network, and
two radio networks – in all, a force to be reckoned with. The
traditional networks just wish that Turner hadn't found that bankrupt station. He has rained down signals that ruined their day.

CNN has become the first global video wire service. It knows the
advantage of staying on the cutting edge with the latest communications equipment. In the Gulf War, a CNN reporter was able to
transmit from Baghdad direct to its own satellite transponder from
an attaché case containing a small satellite dish and transmitter, while
more senior news network reporters were still looking for phone
booths.

The world Turner saw had no national boundaries. Now CNN sweeps into any country, including Canada, without strong resistance. More people are believed to watch CNN in Canada via private satellite dish than watch CBC Newsworld. CNN goes into fifty-five million cable-linked U.S. homes and accounts for 27 percent of all TV news watching. However, CNN is also hard-wired into ten million homes outside the United States, along with 250,000 hotels, embassies, businesses, and stock exchanges. It gathers and repackages news from over 120 countries and relays it into about 100 countries. It's about the only thing that George Bush, Fidel Castro, Lech Walesa, King Hussein, and Saddam Hussein have in common. They all watch it.

Why is CNN now the very profitable ruler of global news gathering? Turner arrived at the mind-shattering conclusion, apparently before others had thought about it, that if he received 150 checks in payment for the same news show, he was better off than if he just did what others were doing and collected one check. Since Turner's organization houses radio and television networks, the same words are frequently used for both television and radio, eliminating duplication in gathering, editing, and dispensing the news in several media simultaneously.

That was Battle One in the Info War. Battle Two is the high-definition struggle for new equipment, transmission techniques, and, most importantly, viewers. After watching this quiet build-up for well over ten years, I think that the Japanese High Definition Television (HDTV) system will win the equipment confrontation, regardless of what the U.S. government attempts to do within its previously defensible borders. The same applies to Canada.

Japan always has the option of acquiring, leasing, or buying a satellite (or a couple of transponders on a satellite) that could blanket North America, thus setting up its own "American" network. You may have noticed that's what Japanese companies have done with their cars and electronic products. I am sure there are countries currently holding unused "rights" to North American satellite slots that would be open to suggestion. Even a satellite now turned to South America could be rotated to broadcast north. When everyone else turns to pay TV, the Japanese might come on strong with all-advertiser-supported television. They do control close to 40 percent of all U.S. movie and TV production.

In transmission techniques the clash is more equal. At the moment satellite transmission has the edge, with the fiber-optic Integrated Services Digital Network (ISDN) expected to be at least an equal power by the end of the decade.

It's the battle for viewers that brings in the Death Stars, satellites so powerful they could put cable companies out of the game and knock down all existing over-air and cable traditional networks and local private and independent TV stations. The shake-up in the advertising world will leave chaos as money streams become blocked, closed, and diverted. What will cause all this disruption? Sky Cable, the largest consortium of all, plans to push 108 channels out of the heavens within two years. All will be high-quality signals directed to small home (or office) dishes. Sky Cable and whatever other direct broadcasting satellite companies try to elbow into the game will all have to offer HDTV to capture a slice of the new pie. Once viewers see HDTV, their old TV sets will become the latest landfill problem.

Not only television can come via these new satellites. You might answer the phone via the TV set; handle banking, shopping, and stock-market manipulations; or read newspapers or magazines via the same route. Fiber-optic networks can match and, in many ways, outperform even the new satellites under some conditions. However, the new Death Star (so nicknamed by fearful cable operators) will likely be locking up customers well before fiber-optic network sales representatives arrive in your neighborhood.

And what about Ted Turner and CNN? He'll be there in one reincarnation or another. No one in the business has his foresight, his daring, or his entrepreneurial ability to change direction.

→   *The Electronic
    Highway*

After World War II, when Germany and then Japan shot ahead in technological skills, remember the remark that those countries "lost the war and won the future"? Now it looks as if the former East Germany will be the first to have the new "electronic highway," or ISDN, delivered directly to home television screens.

Just as some Third World companies leap-frogged some industrialized countries during the past decade, the five eastern states that rejoined the integrated Germany after the collapse of Soviet communism will be first in some aspects of telecommunications. Why? Because they have no status quo to defend, no locked-into-the-past management, no rigid unionized contracts. Their internal communications system, antique by our standards, just doesn't work in today's world. It is far easier to replace the system with a totally new network than to repair it. So this part of Germany will be putting in the newest network, well ahead of the rest of the world. That's the broadband ISDN, a fiber-optic cable network that allows vast amounts of television, facsimile, data, phone, radio, and future broadband multimedia and other communications to travel to any destination the cable takes it. It will also allow computer-based video processing and access to worldwide data banks.

The German version is called FTTH (Fiber to the Home). It is being provided by Telekom Division of the Bundespost, the highly efficient German communications authority. By 1995 the Bundespost hopes to have 1.2 million homes in the former East Germany linked to the system. This is not a market-driven project. The Germans don't even know how much of it will be used. What they do know is that it will be cheaper to lay fiber-optic cable than to try to fix or replace what is there now.

The project is under way in Leipzig, the first test area. The city has a well-educated population that is under-employed. FTTH will provide excellent operational experience and offer participating companies the opportunity to acquire valuable know-how for later transfer of FTTH technology to other areas of the world. Once North America gets around to using ISDN, don't be surprised to find German companies bidding on Canadian or U.S. installations.

→   *Group 4 Faxes*

Most fax machines today transmit at a speed of 9600 baud (one of several electronic transmission speeds). A speed of 9600 baud is equivalent to about a page a minute for Group 3 fax machines. Fax machines have been around since the 1950s, but only in the past decade have they been put into use in large numbers with the arrival of Japanese-made low-cost and high-efficiency units.

Prepare for a faster world. Group 4 transmits at two pages per minute, minimum, up to twenty pages a minute eventually. Group 4 will be the common category with a higher transmission speed for the new fax you will have to purchase once ISDN replaces the current global phone/fax/telegram/telex/cable/TV system. ISDN will enable you to have hundreds of television channels, thousands of radio channels, many electronic magazines and newspapers, and hundreds of business and special service channels. All these will come direct to your home educational/informational/entertainment center. One of these channels will be for the fax service that will travel on these new 56 or 64 kilobits per second lines. At the moment several large users, such as Kodak, Citibank, Merrill Lynch, and the ad agency Young & Rubicam are conducting major tests. John Seazholtz, chairman of the ISDN Executive Committee, says ISDN is "a technology whose time has come."

ISDN will enable subscribers to participate in a video conference across the world at a cost of the phone call plus a slight premium. Northern Telecom, a Canadian company jumping into this rapidly moving field, is making dial-up video conferencing available to its fifty thousand employees at Northern Telecom and its research and development arm, Bell-Northern Research. This will allow anyone in either company to call up others on System 4000, Northern Telecom's worldwide network. System 4000 is currently being installed at sites in Canada, the United States, Europe, and Asia. With it, Northern Telecom's transmission costs have been lowered to $30 per hour from $400 per hour with the previous system. Sending a Group 4 fax via ISDN is eight times faster than at present. If you are working for the post office, plan for an early retirement.

→   *The Fax Box*

Although the principle of the facsimile machine has been around for almost a hundred years and available for almost fifty, it was not until the Japanese reduced the cost and size that the concept went global. Almost overnight, the fax machine became an essential part of business operations around the world.

The type I've been using isn't a fax machine in the usual sense. It is a gray box which, plugged into my Macintosh computer, distinguishes an incoming fax from a call coming from a voice line or from a computer sending E-mail. This fax box also routes calls to its own answering machine when no one is in the office.

The main advantage, apart from a much lower price than the three machines it replaces, is that the fax box uses the higher brain capacity of its attached computer to do all the work done by the expensive (but duplicated, if you have a computer) components in a conventional fax machine. The fax box directs signals from incoming faxes to the computer, which records and stores the information until retrieved. The fax can be read on the computer screen, diverted for permanent storage, printed out, or tossed in the trash – all with a mere click of the mouse (or with your voice, if a Voicewriter II unit is attached).

For outgoing faxes the same system applies in reverse. The fax is prepared on the screen, with pictures if required, then zapped around the world in single or multiple copies at the time designated (for example, after midnight during lowest phone rates). The computer keeps the record until filed, forwarded, or discarded. The same fax box also incorporates its own voice messaging (answering machine) capability. You can even receive a fax and "bounce" its clone worldwide to anyone, again with a few clicks of the mouse. It's so user-friendly, there will eventually be an internal fax box or fax card inside every computer.

The dramatic developments coming with the merger of the computer screen and television will soon provide the latest surprise. For two years now my Digi-TV has been instantly digitizing my television signals from stick antennas, dish, and cable connection and throwing them on my computer screen. From there I can "freeze," alter, store, or forward them anywhere in seconds.

Next year, I will have my computer screen converted to a real time (thirty frames per second), full-color (16.8 million colors), two-way, interactive videophone. Compression Labs Inc. (CLI) of San Jose, California, has succeeded in compressing a mass of data into an area where no technology has gone before. And it will all come over ISDN, the updated fiber-optic phone line. Like the fax box and fax card, this too will eventually fit inside a computer.

→   *Diskfax*

Did you buy one of those bulky desktop fax machines? Then switch to the more compact fax box or even smaller fax card? It's almost time to scrap them. In Hong Kong, Diskfax equipment has been approved for use via the telephone system.

What is Diskfax? The latest method of transferring computer data using ordinary telephone lines. Like the standard fax machine, it eliminates the work of printing and then mailing, at ever-increasing postal rates, information you wish to transfer to another location. Data can be read on a receiving screen ten thousand miles away as clearly as on the dispatching machine screen.

If anything, the process is even simpler than on standard fax machines. All the controls are inside a box 11 inches long and 6.5 inches wide with what looks like a TV controller on top. That's for dialing. Data, graphics, and software are transferred via telephone lines from one floppy disk, inserted into a Diskfax machine at one end, to another floppy disk in a similar machine elsewhere. What was formerly transmitted at a page per minute now moves in one-twentieth the time, three seconds!

Diskfax also eliminates the cost and use of modems that, although tremendously improved in the past two years, still can't really be classified as user-friendly. Poor-quality paper copies are no longer a headache. Encryption is also available for the Diskfax, and a detailed log of transmission action as well as delayed sending capability (to take advantage of lower off-hour rates) are standard.

Diskfax can also cut courier costs: no more shipping across oceans or continents disks or parcels of drawings too big to fit into fax machines. Computer-aided design (CAD) drawings can now be instantly transmitted to any location in the world that has a matching Diskfax machine. The only drawback at the moment is that Diskfax is compatible only with IBM computers (and clones) and the MS-DOS/PC-DOS versions; it has not yet been structured for use with Apple Macintosh computers.

→   *Worldwide*
    Phone Rates

Shortly after the start of the twenty-first century, you will be shopping mostly via catalogs and two-way computers. This will prove so profitable to phone companies (or cable companies if they get there first) that local phone service (to buy all those goodies and make personal calls) will be free. It's going to be possible because of the economically important data you leave in the computer each time you shop. Once that is in place worldwide, flat-rate phone service will follow. Why? There will be almost no extra operational cost to make a direct-dial call from New York across the world to New Delhi via satellite than from New York across the river to New Jersey. Worldwide 800 and 900 numbers will follow.

When Arthur C. Clarke first conceived the idea of geostationary satellites back in 1945, even the word *satellite* meant something else – a celestial body such as a moon. Clarke's concept, outlined clearly (incidentally, it was unpatented) in the October 1945 edition of the British publication *Wireless World,* showed how geostationary satellites would work. Twenty years later the idea was tested by the Soviet Union and led to the more than one thousand geostationary satellites that now orbit our planet.

A phone call, routed through satellite service, reaches its "uplink" point and is directed via microwave toward one of the geostationary satellites (they appear to be stationary because they are rotating at the same apparent speed that the earth rotates), all hovering at an altitude of 22,300 miles above the equator. A satellite can't be anywhere else and be geostationary. Farther out, its velocity would carry it to outer space. Closer in, earth's gravity would eventually draw the satellite closer to earth and it would burn up upon entering the atmosphere. (There are hundreds of other satellites whizzing around up there, but they are not geostationary; they move in elliptical orbits and have shorter life spans.)

The trip up to a communications satellite can start anywhere from Arizona to Zanzibar. Once the signal has gone those 22,300 miles up and back down, the terrestrial distance between caller and receiver is almost irrelevant. So distance becomes irrelevant to the actual operating cost as well.

Some countries will open up their phone companies to such services to keep them in the vanguard of communications innovations. They will develop the system and offer it to the world on a flat-rate, call-anywhere basis. Those that do not offer the same service and join the new global plan will be left behind as technology simultaneously offers small uplink dishes that can tie into such celestial systems independently.

In many ways the change will be reminiscent of the early days of home satellites, when a host of small private companies and entrepreneurs built up a multimillion-dollar industry making and selling satellite dishes for a few thousand dollars. These dishes achieved 95 percent of what was accomplished by the more sophisticated dishes, owned by the phone companies, that then sold for $500,000.

→   *Mobile*
       Satellite Service

Suppose your business partner in Hong Kong has the latest specifications on that new electronic wonder product. The details are too confidential for fax, and it's too complicated and costly to explain over the phone. What to do? Call Low-Earth Orbit Mobile Satellite Service.

LEO MSS satellites – twenty-four of them – will continually circle the globe at an average altitude of 480 miles, arranged in a formation that leaves just seconds between the time one satellite flies out of range of your transceiver and the next unit flies in. (You will almost always be able to contact a LEO satellite, from a vehicle or elsewhere.) You and your Hong Kong colleague have LEO's schedule. She turns on her hand-held ORBCOMM transmitter, weighing under twelve ounces. When LEO comes within range, the computerized hand-held unit zaps up the data (via a simple whip antenna), which is received and held by LEO as the satellite crosses the Pacific at around four thousand miles per hour.

When LEO passes over your city, the transported data is zapped down to your small hand-held or fixed receiver. LEO MSS is also handling thousands, and eventually perhaps millions, of other data packets. LEO satellites are picking up and dropping off messages all the time. Consider them a sort of celestial Federal Express.

The company first into this field is Orbital Sciences Corporation (OSC) of Fairfax, Virginia. Orbital launched its first experimental unit, ORBCOMM-X, from a French rocket that blasted off in 1991 from Kourou, French Guiana. It is orbiting successfully, but an uncorrected glitch has so far prevented the unit from communicating with OSC scientists. The problem will eventually be solved or another unit will be launched. When operating, this will be the first practical, satellite-to-individual commercial use of Very High Frequency (VHF).

ORBCOMM's hand-held emergency terminal will allow flyers, hunters, explorers, and ordinary travelers to "keep in touch." Costs for expensive search-and-rescue operations should be greatly reduced once those light, hand-held units are in universal distribution. LEO will also be able to monitor moving boxcars, ocean buoys, highway traffic, containers, and hazardous materials; track animals; contact trucks or emergency vehicles; collect and distribute weather data; monitor river levels; watch your cottage in the country; or beam down directions to a friend in a wheelchair. LEO will do all this using less than one megahertz of bandwidth in the broadcast spectrum.

First to sign a tie-in agreement with ORBCOMM to market the service was the largest power corporation in Venezuela, which provides electricity to more than five million people in Caracas. According to OSC, interest from various Canadian sources is high but there are no firm deals as yet. ORBCOMM has applied for Pioneer Preference Status from the U.S. Federal Communications Commission (FCC), which would, if the FCC's new rules are adopted, provide preferential status for ORBCOMM under the new procedural rules.

→   *Satellite Dishes*

The only problem with the newest satellite dish is that it's so small you may lose it. Satellite CD Radio recently conducted its first public demonstration of a digital audio broadcast to be delivered via satellite with CD quality to a consumer antenna. The patch antenna that will be used when the service is up and running will be two inches square, about the size of a business card. The antenna can sit on a window sill or be mounted on an automobile under the paint. These antennas might even end up in caps for joggers and walkers. The antennas will allow reception even when cars are moving at high speed or partially shrouded by trees or similar obstructions, thus eliminating the signal breakup and "multipathing" common to current radio.

It's the same technology used during the Gulf War. Remember the days when it took sixty-five years from invention to universal distribution, as in the case of the electric motor? Now it takes mere months. Eventually the minidishes should be able to handle 120 channels, but initially the service would probably only offer 30 to 60 channels. Such channels can be allotted for regional or nationwide audiences.

The new satellite that will be transmitting such fare will be more powerful, using fifty watts of power at 2.3 gigahertz. That's ten times more power than contained in the original television satellites. The FCC only recently announced the allocation of such a frequency. Dolby technology will handle the digital processing.

"Narrowcasting" a series of programs is much like many of the new special interest magazines in print. The idea is that a satellite will attract those whose numbers, in any one city, are not large enough to warrant a special interest local station. They would only garner an audience large enough to be profitable when people with a specific interest were listening all over a country or continent – such groups as bird-watchers, dog-lovers, pigeon-breeders, tropical fish fanciers, or electric train aficionados. You tune not by station, frequency, or city, but by format. Listeners also get a constant window on their radio displaying information – for example, with music, they would get the artist, song, format, and channel.

Satellite CD Radio says its operational charge for the "owner" of any particular channel would be about $100 per transmission hour. No doubt those who take a twenty-four-hour-a-day, year-round contract would get a substantial discount. Radios able to receive the new frequency (*not* AM or FM) are not yet built, but Satellite CD Radio expects about one million vehicle and home/office receivers to be manufactured by 1995. Proposals for construction of the new satellite will be issued as soon as the FCC issues the construction permit.

The next development in satellite dishes? Imagine you're on the beach at Atlantic City. A couple comes by and sits down close to you. The young man has been carrying what looks like a cafeteria serving tray with a handle on it. He sets it down, flicks open an easel-type stand, and turns the unit toward the southern sky. The material on the face of this tray is composed of new solar cell material that is converting sunlight into electrical power. It is also picking up signals from one of the satellites hovering over the equator. One-quarter of the tray lights up with a five-inch television picture!

No battery. No wall plug. The satellite receiver and solar generator are contained in the same compact unit. Look for it on your electronic store shelf within three years. And yes, you guessed it. It's Japanese.

→   *The Latest Phones*

Remember the standard black phone? Now, of course, we have cordless, cellular, and speaker phones, along with answering machine phones, fax-phones, and other multiple units that handle phone, fax, and voice messaging all at once. What's next? Those who want everything can have their own individual "phone company," a unit that does what the phone company does. It's expensive today, but within five years it will be as cheap as the first cellular phones.

The MagnaPhone, a portable satellite telephone, is the most compact and lightweight single-case Inmarsat-A, Class 1 Satellite Communications (SATCOM) terminal available. It provides telephone, fax, telex, and data communications anywhere in the world. The carrying case travels as airline luggage. It is an automatic and programmable land earth station. It can handle multiple phone support (up to five connectors), and operates with any two-wire touch-tone phone. It's self-testing, and has system status reporting and a voice synthesizer.

The most compact unit currently available, it is less than two cubic feet, including the antenna, but it weighs forty-seven pounds. Open the case and minutes later you are in operation. I love the directions: "Remove from case, unfold legs, swing umbrella antenna into place. Turn it on, aim [at the satellite]." The antenna is about three feet long when extended for operation.

The MagnaPhone selects the closest land earth station near the call destination site automatically. It can be programmed to handle thirty user-assigned country codes, provides a four-line by forty character LCD display, speakerphone, handset, and keyboard. Also included are all those things normally expected on a phone: redial, number storage, speed dialing, and external telephone intercom; an attachable thermal printer is also available. The unit permits the use of slow-scan video, computers, modems, remote radio repeaters, encryption, and other devices.

If you don't need your own earth station but want the latest in phones, Motorola's CT2 is it. This phone weighs only 6.6 ounces, fits into a shirt pocket, can operate for ten continuous hours or one hundred hours standby time on disposable batteries. It is rechargeable with a separate nickel-cadmium battery unit.

The CT2 designation stands for cordless telephone second generation. It is digital rather than analog, giving superior voice quality, less interference, and better security. It could be the phone you keep for life. Imagine: the same number from womb to tomb, and it will work almost anywhere in the world. With this phone you can give up your fixed, wired phone if you so desire.

In cities such as Singapore and Hong Kong, CT2 is, in some cases, completely replacing the old-fashioned wired phone. At home or in the office it is a cordless. But the great new feature is that when you roam around town, it still works, providing limited-range wireless communications via telepoints – industrial robotic relays – just like a cordless base station. As long as CT2 is within range of one of these repeaters, calls will be relayed into the phone system to anywhere in the world. Singapore already has thirty-five hundred repeaters in place and another fifteen hundred scheduled for installation. Hong Kong will end up with about the same number.

The Motorola Silverlink 2000 is already available in the United Kingdom, France, Germany, Spain, Thailand, and Malaysia. Note that North America is no longer first with the latest technology into service. Government red tape and telephone monopolies are holding back communications in a fashion that would make India, the original home of red tape, proud.

The cost is but a fraction of cellular service. What makes this phone inherently inexpensive is its ability to use Public Switched Telephone Network (PSTN) infrastructure rather than creating a new, expensive system such as cellular phones have needed. It also uses low-power handsets. It is not meant to replace cellular, except in a limited way. Silverlink 2000 cannot be used in a car while it is moving or in rural areas (as yet) because it does not have the "hand-over" ability that goes with a cellular phone that keeps reconnecting you as you move from cell to cell in the system. But that is also its main cost-saving feature. CT2 is restricted to about the same range from its base repeater station as a present home cordless allows.

Currently, CT2 does not receive voice calls. You can only make outgoing calls, but it does have the ability to tie in with satellite and other paging services. A small window on the phone displays the calling number; so if you phone that caller right away, he or she will think you are receiving messages via thought waves. The system is that fast. Soon CT2 systems will offer various forms of two-way calling as well.

Licenses have been granted to four companies in Canada. In the United States, standards are still under debate. Once this system is in place, the reputation of Canadians and other North Americans as the world's most frequent phone callers will jump another notch.

Installed telepoint networks provide two, four, or six telephone line capability multiplexed over forty voice channels in one indoor/outdoor cabinet, network control center, and business management/billing system. A business can use such a system as, in effect, its own private phone company by installing its own telepoint stations in appropriate locations.

Further developments? New infrared built-in transmitters on a phone made by Tek Communications open up another world. This phone offers aspects of both cordless and cellular for a fraction of the cost. The technology is so effective that every car would have one, if our phone companies didn't have monopolies.

You're driving home. It's raining and cold, and you want to phone home to say you will be late. You see a pay phone by the road. You plug the infrared phone into the cigarette lighter, punch in your home number and your credit card number, and sit back in the comfort and security of your car.

How does this new phone work? Infrared signals powered by the car battery are relayed to a chip in the pay phone telling it to take an incoming signal from the Tek phone. Your signal is processed in the same manner as if you were standing in the booth, but it bypasses the coin slot. The Tek phone is one of the many better ideas that come along when monopolies fall.

In Canada, the federal government's obsession with control via the status-quo Canadian Radio-television and Telecommunications Commission (CRTC) has held the country back – so much that by the time deregulation hits, Canadians probably won't have the know-how required to manufacture, sell, distribute, and operate the newest equipment. No other country in the world has seen such a leading position in communications deteriorate as rapidly as the national debt has multiplied. Expect a Japanese satellite over Canada in future, offering a deal that Canadian TV viewers and radio listeners won't be able to refuse.

Finally, new technologies have made possible a phone that listens. Yell "Police" and it will dial them. Murmur your husband's name and there he is. Say "Tax collection" and it disconnects. It's called the Voiceprint phone.

Voiceprint can dial fifty contacts and record the names of people and companies called, the length of conversation, and the dates of the last hundred phone calls. Say goodbye to conventional directories and card files. To use the phone, say the name of the person or company you want to call. The LED window displays the name and number and Voiceprint dials the number automatically. Touch a single key and emergency numbers are automatically dialed.

When you program the phone, it analyzes your voice, creates a unique voiceprint of each name programmed into the telephone, and then stores the information. The phone can be programmed in any language.

→   *Satellite Stock*
       Quotations

You're standing on a street corner. A young woman opens her purse and pulls out what appears to be the familiar pocket calculator. She punches in some numbers, then whips out a concealed antenna and looks at the result. Has she just figured out her bank balance? Some months ago in Chicago she might have been one of the first with the new Quotrek communications system.

This is how it works. Back in New York the NYSE, AMEX, and NASDAQ stock exchanges and the CME, CBT, and CEC commodity markets provide a real-time data stream to their west coast computer control center. These familiar stock exchanges are sending out their up-to-the-femtosecond stock and commodity price information. Such data is encoded and processed by high-speed VAX computers and transmitted from a local earth station uplink (pending completion of the fiber-optic link and a teleport on Staten Island). Messages are narrow-beamed to Western Union's Westar IV satellite over the equator. The signal is then wide-beamed down to selected FM radio stations in major cities across North America.

That was no calculator in the woman's hand. It was a lightweight cordless receiver with programmable memory and forty-character liquid crystal screen. It decodes, processes (at up to thirty thousand bits per second), and displays updates within seconds of the transactions on the exchange floor.

The unit weighs less than a pound, can monitor seven thousand stocks (a review of the "loop" of all those stocks takes just forty-five seconds), and can give instant review of a personal portfolio along with privacy, flexibility, and convenience. You can even take it to bed. Meanwhile, your local FM station still plays music, with "side-channel" broadcasts to Quotrek units within a thirty to forty mile range of its station. It's another example of various communications devices and systems "marrying" to produce newer, more versatile offspring.

8

Japan

→   *Japanese Rule*

As they lead the world into the twenty-first century, the Japanese have an educated and sophisticated citizenry, understand that information is the "ore" of the future, and are fast learning how to mine it. Canada is spending 50 percent more per capita for half the education that students are getting in Japan. Yet the Japanese are not satisfied and are changing their system. The next sixteen universities to be built in Japan will be private. The Japanese are also more attuned to global competition. In an information society, those with the best information usually win.

What enables the Japanese to move so quickly? For starters, they have a far higher literacy rate than we do in North America. In the United States about 20 percent of the people are illiterate and another 20 percent are functionally illiterate. In Japan, with a more complex language, the rate is 1 percent. Tests conducted in nineteen countries by the United Nations placed Japanese students at the top.

American students were fifteenth. Tests conducted in 1982 by the British psychologist Richard Lynn showed Japanese children averaging IQs of 111. Half the American students rated under 100. Even more embarrassing was Lynn's estimate that only 2 percent of American kids had IQs of 130 or more. At least 10 percent of Japanese students exceeded that level.

To aid that high literacy level, Japanese book publishers turn out thirty-five thousand new titles a year. That is twice as many per capita as in the United States. And the Japanese read what they buy. Book clubs have never caught on in Japan; it seems the Japanese don't buy what they don't read. In North America hardly anyone reads Japanese authors, either in original or translated versions. Meanwhile most worthwhile books available in North America or Europe are also for sale in Japan – in English or Japanese. The Japanese are more aware than we are of what is happening in other countries, especially in science, technology, and economics.

About 93 percent of all Japanese regularly read newspapers, more per capita than any other country except Sweden. Circulation figures in Japan are astronomical. *Ashai Shimbun* sells 7.5 million and *Mainichi Shimbun* 8.7 million – per edition! Their staffs total eight to ten thousand per paper. They have their own aircraft fleets. They blanket the world.

Japan also has more than three thousand magazines. They are not all "intellectual," of course, but there is such a wide variety that a sizable segment of the Japanese public is continually exposed to sophisticated interpretations of complex problems. And their JISO satellite TV transmissions, emanating from either New York or Washington, provide more in-depth information than most North American TV broadcasts.

The Japanese have fifteen hundred Very High Frequency (VHF) stations and ten thousand Ultra-High Frequency (UHF) stations. Most are operated by NHK, Japan's version of the BBC. Half of NHK's stations produce only educational and cultural programming. Even stations classified as "general interest" devote less than 30 percent of their time to entertainment. The 470 VHF and 2,900 UHF private stations that are mainly entertainment-oriented are licensed on the proviso that they devote 30 percent of their time to educational and cultural programming.

Japanese news programs are, according to Robert C. Christopher, former senior editor of *Newsweek* and *Time* and author of *The Japanese Mind*, "superior in depth and thoughtfulness to those offered by the major U.S. networks. NHK news staff drive hard for objectivity [while] there is more and better backgrounding than U.S. television offers. NHK also supplies most Japanese classrooms with TV sets and publishes hundreds of thousands of textbooks to accompany the educational TV programs.

I could fill the rest of this book with statistics related to Japan in the information society. One example: there are more telephones in Japan than in all of Africa, Southeast Asia, and Russia combined. The explosion of fax machines has forced the Japanese to increase telephone numbers to eight digits to handle the demand for new numbers.

What lies behind Japan's global leadership in the late stages of the second millennium? Simply put, the Japanese know the value of up-to-date information.

→   *Auto Imports –*
      Phase Two

Not long ago, North American auto manufacturers held 85 percent of the world automobile market. Today it's down to 35 percent and falling. Already Japanese cars account for 40 percent of all the cars sold on the West Coast of North America – 50 percent in some areas. By the end of 1995, the Japanese will control half of all North American car sales. They are now preparing to shift into "Phase Two."

When that occurs, the former Big Three North American manufacturers will probably see one of their members, likely Chrysler, fade from the scene. What's left will be the "Big Four": General Motors,

Ford, Honda, and Toyota. North America won't be able to buy what they will collectively produce. Another company will have to go and it will not be Honda or Toyota.

The Japanese car manufacturing industry is now thinking "best packaging." This attitude incorporates attractiveness, sensitivity to the customer, and concern for the environment. It stresses the slogan of an earlier decade: "small is beautiful." To show how big their small thinking is, Nippondenso Co. Ltd., a major Japanese maker of car electronics, produced a display containing cars 0.2 inches long with glass wheels, which race along a display track. They contain motors smaller than a grain of rice. Nippondenso is not just watching the highways of the world's traffic systems but also human highways of blood circulation. An even-smaller model traveling in the blood-stream could one day clean up plugged blood vessels.

Mitsubishi Motors Corp. has developed "concept" cars that appear to be the big-brother version to that Italian hit of the 1950s, the Lambretta scooter. With environmental pressure mounting, the Japanese realize that the market will eventually insist on further emission reductions. They want to be ready. Are you aware that today's small motorbikes emit fifty times more exhaust per horse-power than standard automobiles?

Don't be fooled by what appear today to be toys. Mitsubishi's mS.1000 car has solar-induced air conditioning. It reacts to the sun, starts the cooling unit, and powers the unit with the sun's rays. The car remains cool even when parked in the sun, and upholstery lasts longer. The paint, which is energy-efficient, can change from magenta pink to beige when the temperature rises above 80°F and dispose of the heat, unless it is required in the winter.

Meanwhile, Nissan Motor Co. Ltd. has a six-seater "Cocoon" built for senior citizens. Ever been inconvenienced by losing your car keys? The Cocoon can read your fingerprint, which was coded into the car at delivery. The car will open on command — but just for you. Knowing some seniors' propensity for a quick snooze, the car will contain a buzzer that keeps drivers awake. The buzzer will also activate a steering wheel that emits an aroma that enhances alertness.

As the highways of the planet become more crowded, and governments are increasingly strapped to upgrade infrastructures, Japanese car manufacturers know small will continue to pay off. Smaller cars mean more parking space, more space on highways, and less fuel consumption. The day may come in some countries when governments may be forced to mandate car size for both space and gas consumption. The Japanese small-car strategy is to build on a utilitarian chassis. Frills can then be added at minimal cost.

Thinking smaller "speeds up the entire evolution of the company," according to Tokyo-based Douglas Kennedy, an industry expert. It will allow the Japanese to turn out new cars in half a year rather than the traditional North American cycle of three to four years.

→ *Advanced*
   Materials

Within ten years, new houses won't be made just of wood or bricks. Cars and engines won't be made of steel. Airplanes won't be constructed of riveted aluminum sheet metal. Leisure sports equipment will be composed of materials that don't exist today. This revolution doesn't bode well for North American or European business. Natural resources, as we have known them, will no longer be required in anywhere near the quantities they have been in the past.

The new structural materials are classified as ceramics, polymers, or metals. Now two or more of these materials are being combined to form composites that have superior properties to those of their constituent materials. These advanced materials are known as matrix composites – ceramic (CMC), polymer (PMC), and metal (MMC). Also entering this field are other metal alloys and unreinforced engineering plastics, all called *advanced materials*.

The new materials are stronger, weigh less, and can endure far higher temperature ranges – up to 30,000°F – than other materials. They may lend themselves to automated production techniques in ways not possible with Industrial Age raw materials. At the moment they are more expensive and difficult to fabricate, but that is about to change as a whole new discipline known as processing science develops. Calculations show that an automobile body containing 250 to 350 parts could be reduced, using PMCs, to something like ten parts. The result: less labor, faster production, more appeal, and built-in efficiency.

Canadian and American companies tend to be "pulled by the market." Until there appears to be strong consumer, industrial, or commercial demand for a product, they hesitate to invest in research and development or to prepare for volume production. In the case of these advanced materials, North American and European manufacturers foresee no substantial developments for ten to twenty years. They fear that new products may not be viable in the short term and that any investment during that time will be lost. Because their citizens have a low savings rate (in the United States now about 2 percent of gross income), money costs more than in Japan. North American companies are also forced to consider shareholders who are fickle and may depart if the next quarter shows no profit. Such companies might easily be taken over while money is tied up in future programs.

The Japanese, on the other hand, believe in "technology push." They think that if they create a new product and research the market intensively, they can force consumption by pushing the new advantages built into their latest product. By getting in not at the ground floor but at the excavation, they can achieve shorter development times.

The Japanese are also willing to sacrifice near-term profits to gain the production experience necessary to secure a sizable share of future markets. Shareholders see the advantage of long-term market share and forgo short-term profit for the larger capital gains to be made when the new market explodes. Their high savings rate of the past decade (averaging around 22 percent of gross income) lets Japanese companies borrow at low interest rates for new ventures. This philosophy has worked in the past with videocassette recorders, television, microchips, fax machines, and automobiles. Think it won't work in the future with advanced materials?

→   *Square Logs*

When I visited lumber mills and lumber retail outlets in Japan, I was impressed with the way the Japanese handle logs. By contrast, we appear to butcher and mutilate our timber. They treasure, enhance, and beautify it. I saw Japanese technicians study a log for hours before they decided how to cut it. When they did cut it, the waste material would fit in one hand. Many Japanese lumber mills cut only one log a day. They make more profit from that one log than some of our mills make on hundreds of trees.

Now the Japanese are going even further. They have decided that round logs have more value when they are turned into square logs. That way the largest amount of waste – that lost in trimming a round log until it is square, and then converting it into two-by-fours or whatever – is eliminated.

Scientist Yoshinori Kabayashi of the Nara Prefectural Forest Experiment Station near Osaka invented and developed a process that "cooks" round logs until they are square. The technique is startlingly simple. In his specially designed microwave "oven," the temperature of the log is raised to 250°F, thereby making the round log so pliable it can be massaged into the desired square shape. The log is allowed to cool to room temperature while still in the press process. Then it is heated again to the same temperature. The process does not damage wood fibers, but actually makes them stronger, denser, and less subject to warping or splitting. The specific gravity of the square log, its hardness, and its resistance to abrasion are all superior to that of the raw log. The pressure required to achieve the square profile is surprisingly low – as low as 150 pounds per square inch. The log retains its square shape when released from the oven and the conversion pressure.

During the squaring process, as the logs are compressed, a considerable amount of water is ejected, usually about five quarts from a three-foot-long cedar log. The resulting log is firmer and denser; it has been bumped into a higher-grade quality. After the process, the quality of a cedar log approximates that of the more expensive Japanese cypress. According to a Canadian expert, that could turn a $70 log into a $210 product. How's that for value added? According to Kobayashi the possibilities do not stop there. Crooked, misshapen, and distorted logs, which in our forests today would be discarded or relegated to the chip pile, can be straightened and squared.

Because of its size, the microwave oven used in the laboratory process has been used to test only short sections of logs. Such an oven constructed to handle commercial lengths of timber in sixteen-foot lengths is estimated to cost about $150,000, a relatively minor expense. The implications could be industry-shattering. If the Japanese find it economic to supply all of their 300,000 sawmills with factory-produced industrial models of this equipment, they could substantially increase the value of any log. Competing companies around the world would be left behind.

The Japanese may agree to export their revolutionary log compressor – at their price, and after they have supplied their own country – to friendly countries first. For now, though, the Nara prefectural government is not allowing anyone else to use the patent. It appears that Nara officials want companies in their prefecture to receive first opportunities. "After one or two years," says Kobayashi, "it will probably sell licenses for the technology outside the prefecture."

→   *Economics
of Scope*

One Japanese construction company has probably spent more on research and development in residential construction during the last decade than the entire Canadian residential building industry has during the last century. The Misawa Corporation, the largest home builder in the world with well over 350,000 houses built the old way, is now producing ceramic homes at its Nagoya plant. These homes are guaranteed for twenty years, require no fire insurance, and incorporate technologies and research findings unknown in the west. To put it simply, sand (silicon and limestone) goes in one end of the production plant and a house comes out the other. On-site erection time is around 2.5 hours. The three-story houses run from twelve hundred to eighteen hundred square feet.

More importantly, Misawa has conquered "economies of scope." These are not the economies of scale of the Industrial Age – whereby you can make ten thousand identical homes more cheaply per unit than you can make ten – but economies of scope that permit the construction of ten thousand *different* homes at almost the same price per house that it costs to produce ten thousand identical homes! It's all in the computer software and the five-story production building. Refrigerators in these homes are still in the kitchen, but the irritating hum of the motor has been removed – and placed in the garage, where the heat from the motor keeps the car warm. Other features include fiber-optic cabling for the home computer system and sensors that exchange shower humidity for cooler, dryer outside air when required.

In the commercial construction of hotels, office buildings, and apartments, another astonishing development has come from the Ohbayashi Corporation of Osaka. They build the first floor of such buildings, and then that floor (in reality a robot) builds the rest of the structure! The only humans constantly involved in the actual building process are those in the control tower monitoring computer operations – operations that continue twenty-four hours a day, every day of the year, uninterrupted by labor or weather problems. Think of the dramatic savings in short-term financing costs alone.

In another development, the La Foret Engineering and Information Service Company of Tokyo has already provided seventy-five installations worldwide (most in Japan) with their *himawari*

(Japanese for sunflower) zero-voltage interior illumination system. The company has erected satellite-like rotating dishes that each contain a packed cluster of Fresnel lenses. These dishes follow the movement of the sun, collecting and intensifying sunlight and feeding it through fiber-optic cables to building interiors. Along the way they subject the light to a "light-shift," removing the harmful ultraviolet rays, converting the infrared to heat if desired, and bringing only "pure" sunlight to the people and plants in the buildings. The benefits? Cheaper cabling, lower insurance, much longer cable runs without power boosters, a cleaner, maintenance-free installation, and no risk of short circuits. I don't know of a single North American construction company taking advantage of this technologically superior system.

→ *Robotic
Construction*

The arrival of robots and automation on the factory floor signaled the beginning of the decline of union power. Computers marched into the office and increased the productivity of (remaining) office workers. Now comes the most dramatic production development yet – office buildings, apartments, and hotels built by a robot.

As mentioned, Ohbayashi Corporation introduced early in 1990 the world's first virtually workerless automatic construction machine. Robots have been used in the Japanese construction industry for some time, but only the single job/single robot type. Ohbayashi's revolutionary concept involves robotization of the entire construction system. Known as the Fully Automatic Building Construction System (FABCS), it is protected under six patents.

All components of the new building – pillars, beams, external wall panels, internal partitions, ceilings, floor slabs, and other units – are factory-produced to precise specifications. Components are stored in a warehouse near the assembly site or underneath the robot machine. Inside the warehouse, self-propelled stacker cranes convey components horizontally or vertically to position. As assembly progresses, preprogrammed cranes retrieve the right parts at the right time and stack them on conveyor cars.

The heart of the system is the Super Construction Floor (SCF), an automated factory with walls and a roof. Identical numbers of pillars are located at the exact spot and angle as called for in the building design. Each pillar contains a hydraulic cylinder, which supports the SCF and lifts it up to the next level when a floor has been completed.

Inside the SCF, overhead cranes cover the entire floor. Each crane has its own complement of robots: assembly robots, welding robots, inspection robots, exterior panel installation robots, interior component placement robots, and so forth. Robots and cranes are computer-controlled from the control room on top of the SCF, assuring precision and accuracy in placement and assembly. Self-propelled conveyor cars and elevators carry components and materials automatically to the assembly site.

When the SCF starts first-floor assembly, hydraulic cylinders on its pillars are extended so the SCF stands one story off the ground. When pillars transported by crane to the assembly point arrive, all the original pillars retract individually into the SCF, making room for the new pillar. The pillar is then welded to the base by the welding robot.

When all pillars are attached, beams, floor slabs, wall panels, and interior material are automatically added by the overhead cranes and their associated robots. Once the floor is complete, the hydraulic cylinders are extended, raising the SCF up one more floor. The process is repeated until the building is completed.

Completely workerless, the FABCS is not subject to labor shortages or disruptions. Dangerous work is done by the robots, so on-site safety is enhanced, with no workers' compensation premiums or claims necessary. The temporary structures and scaffolding required is limited. Noise pollution on the site is minimal. Operations are not affected by adverse weather conditions. Working seven days a week, twenty-four hours a day, these nonstop operations result in rapid completion and lower financing costs. Prefabricated components and materials mean increased precision and quality. Design, estimates, and execution are done through the Computer-aided Design and Computer-aided Manufacturing (CAD/CAM) system. The fabrication of such components will create new industries.

Ohbayashi points out that each building must be designed with this type of automated construction in mind. Each floor must be the same size, but varying interiors are possible. Most economical are high-rise buildings that require repeated executions of the same procedures. Thus, high-rise residential buildings, office buildings, and hotels are the most appropriate uses.

Ohbayashi considers the FABCS just the beginning. Long-range plans include even taller high-rise buildings and eventually construction of a lunar city. This company is thinking ahead. North America, meanwhile, steadfastly refuses to keep pace. Last year alone the Japanese installed more robots than have been installed in all of North America since robots were first developed.

→   *Island of*
              Innovation

Here's an example of the creativity that made America great in the past, but which is now more common in Asia. A "convertible" building has opened in Tokyo. Owned by IBA Inc. of Japan, the building is a hotel by night and offices by day. The basic business of hotels, of course, is providing overnight accommodation for travelers. IBA found the daytime emptiness unproductive and unnerving. What to do? IBA decided to end the hotel operations in the morning when most travelers leave and do a fast conversion to daytime office space. Nighttime beds are transformed into office couches, and secretarial help and office equipment replace room service and the ever-present Japanese massage.

Does the constant stream of hotel guests and office personnel ever get confusing? A simple solution prevents that. The magnetic hotel-entrance card won't let guests into hotel rooms until darkness falls. An early morning wake-up call gets them moving. (If you sleep in too late, you might wake up and wonder if you're dreaming.) In reality, of course, staff make sure rooms are ready well in advance of the switch. A hotel that last year grossed $5 million has almost doubled its gross income.

Another Japanese innovation is the artificial "island." This huge edifice, being designed by the Taisei Corporation of Tokyo in the shape of a seagull (and named "Jonathan Livingston Seagull"), will operate from a single-point mooring system adaptable to water depths from 150 to 500 feet. Engineering ensures that the island will always face oncoming wave action regardless of changing wind direction.

Such mobility guarantees that the sixteen fish farms located in the lee of the construction "wings" will always be in calm waters. The constantly changing ocean habitat will closely resemble the natural wild fish habitat. This prevents the pollution prevalent in the slow-moving waters of most shore-based fish farms, which can cause oxygen-deprivation, algal bloom confinement, and other ills. Expensive feeding costs associated with land-based, coastal fish farms will be eliminated because natural water-borne food will flow continuously through the fish farms of the artificial island.

The $450 million structure is about the size of ten jumbo jets. Floor space covers 560,000 square feet on eight floors, three of them below sea level. The island will contain a one thousand-room hotel with connected shopping arcade, convention center, marina, aquarium, and the world's first floating in-house sightseeing submarine base. It will also incorporate an ocean research institute, entertainment facilities, and a heliport. A pier twenty-six hundred feet long is designed to accommodate eighty fishing boats, and two hundred rooms will accommodate their crews.

The structure is large enough to ride out, in relative calm, the typhoons prevalent in the seas surrounding Japan. In fact, the higher the seas, the lower the operating cost. A wave power extractor and electrical generators, which will always face the wind, will absorb energy from oncoming waves and convert it into electrical power for the floating island while reducing the height of the waves. Overall island movement is estimated to be less than half an inch, even in waves up to ten feet high. Propulsion units will provide a steadying influence against changing tidal currents, waves, and wind.

→   *Tokyo's Underland*

That's not the end of the Taisei Corporation's original initiatives. Besides artificial islands, the company is a pioneer in the development of underground facilities. When land cost was in the millions per acre, it cost two to three times as much to build underground as on the surface, so few did. Not long ago an acre of land sold in Tokyo for more than a billion dollars, which means building underground is now relatively cheap, an idea whose time has come.

The Taisei Corporation has designed the self-contained "Alice City" (as in Lewis Carroll's *Alice in Wonderland*), an underground metropolis designed for the twenty-four-hour-a-day twenty-first century. With the Taisei plan, underground space can be effectively used for many purposes. For instance, there are a large number of above-ground installations that would be more effective underground, such as power stations, warehouses, railway yards, and some specialized manufacturing facilities. The plan does not stop there. It calls for an elaborate infrastructure, including office and town space. In the infrastructure areas, the plan includes power generation, regional heating, waste recycling, and sewage treatment facilities. Such underground space can be spherical or cylinder-shaped.

Office space will house business operations, shopping malls, hotels, theaters, and sports arenas. Express elevators or an extension of an underground railway system will run to the bottom level. Solar domes or atrium space will eliminate any feeling of claustrophobia.

As some office, commercial, and entertainment areas move underground, a ten-minute vertical commute may replace a two-hour run from the Tokyo suburbs.

An underground city has many advantages. Heating costs for the entire city are almost totally eliminated, along with the resulting pollution. The constant natural underground temperature allows the heat provided by the city's inhabitants and machines to be collected, filtered, vented, and sold to the buildings above ground at competitive rates.

Underground space is ideal for any city's infrastructure from the standpoints of isolation, sound insulation, and earthquake resistance. A side benefit is the preservation of the above-ground environment. How will people deal with the "depressing" feeling associated with subterranean development? Anyone who has seen the $2,500-a-second computer-generated graphics at Toronto's underground "Tour of the Universe" theater knows that you can very quickly forget you are underground when such holographic-type vistas are visible outside the window.

Construction costs have been carefully studied: a twelve-floor office space (260 feet deep) would cost about $577 million, and a 260-foot diameter and 200-foot-high infrastructure space with its base placed 530 feet below ground would run about $692 million. Total cost for a city of 100,000 inhabitants is estimated at $4 billion. A lot of money, you say? It's rumored to be roughly half the asking price of one other surface acre on Tokyo's Ginza strip!

To the Japanese, who have unbridled enthusiasm for the twenty-first century, underground development means more than just a few projects in their own country for today and tomorrow. They are well aware that the world population is going to continue to increase considerably before it slows down. Mexico City, for example, is projected to reach a population of thirty million within a decade. Other world centers face similar problems. With the experience gained in building the world's first underground cities, who will have the engineering know-how to capture such contracts when other world cities reach the density and land costs that make underground development economic? The Japanese, of course, whose actions today are usually based on their understanding of tomorrow.

→   *Ski Tokyo?*

Kazunobu Abe, chief architect for the huge Kajima Corporation, has sent me the outline, plans, and pictures for his new artificial reality "indoor skiing resort." It's called Urban Slalom, and there's nothing in the world like it. How would you like to try "hot-dogging" on the moon – or over Manhattan – or even through a tropical plantation? Technology makes it possible.

Abe is building a mountain in downtown Tokyo. He's putting a 200-foot-high, 30,000-square-foot building over it (with a floor area of 100,000 square feet) and making it snow inside! It will be an all-season, all-weather indoor ski resort in the heart of one of the world's most expensive, bustling cities. (Another is also planned for Osaka.) It will be a recreational resort to boggle the imagination.

Years ago, at the Boeing Research Center in Seattle, I "flew" the Lunar Lander in a simulated setting. It was an off-world version of the flight simulator used by major airlines to train air crews. The seeming "reality" of the experience can only be appreciated at first hand. Urban Slalom will be a further outgrowth of the same illusionary technique.

With the Japanese government urging its legendarily hard-working citizens to increase their leisure time and activities, and with economic, health, and social indicators worldwide pointing to increased attention to lifestyle, Abe is clearly onto something. And he is not limiting his scope to his own country. The plan could easily be adapted to the Caribbean or Saudi Arabia.

Urban Slalom has three ski runs (at least one with a sixteen-hundred-foot straight or spiral path). All have a base of five to eight inches of scientifically controlled powder snow laid down by nine machines.

Using the latest reflection techniques (spatial dramatization), resortlike (and other) images will show on the surrounding walls. Courses of varying lengths and slope angles – 5° to 30° – provide introductory, intermediate, and advanced courses. Lifts quickly carry skiers back to the top of the "mountain" for maximum skiing time. The complex also includes fashion, gourmet, and physical fitness facilities. But the highlight may be a swimming pool that you can ski right into! Also included will be a communications salon and a golf school and driving range.

The Kajima Corporation hopes to create a sports complex that is an extension of everyday life, not something people would do just for a week or a couple of weekends a year, but that would make skiing in downtown Tokyo more like playing tennis or going to the theater. Skiing would become a sport where most of your time is spent enjoying your leisure, not fighting traffic trying to get to the slopes. One key marketing target group is middle-aged women, who in Japan now have the money and time to do what they couldn't in their earlier years.

The themes stressed time and again in Abe's plans and promotional material are quality and service. I expect the world will beat a path to his door, but he probably won't be home. He'll be out pushing the concept worldwide. I bet you'll find one of these artificial reality resorts in many of the world's major cities by the start of the third millennium.

→   *Robotized Stores*

Think robotized supermarkets are a thing of the future? The Japanese supermarket chain Seiyu is already into the tenth year of operation of its ultra computerized store – the first in the world – in the Nokendai section of Tokyo. The store features standard high technology: automated billing, accounting, inventory control, and robots to handle the merchandise. But would you expect an

"Information Salon" where parents can leave their children while they shop? Kids can learn English in a "Star Words" game or be guided by an actual Masai chief (on a laser videodisk system) in a search for animals in "Jungle Game." Children as young as three, along with their sometimes computer-illiterate parents, are introduced to the educational uses of computers and knowledge-enhancing videodisks. The salon also has a piano-playing robot, and another robot that puts jigsaw puzzles together.

The concept could change retailing forever. According to Seiyu President Seiji Tsutsumi, the focus is now where it belongs: "on the person-to-person relationship between customer and retailer." Clerks now actually help the shopper instead of carrying crates of lettuce or stacking shelves. No humans are involved in that process. Everything from unloading trucks to stocking shelves is done at night, by robot, when the store is empty. Videotapes of the robots' night actions are played for customers' education the next day. The stockroom keeps track of every sale, re-ordering according to past demands based on day, time, season, and product.

The automated process begins outside. The parking robot opens the gate and hands you a magnetic-tape parking card. If you hold a credit card from the supermarket's parent company, Saison, you require no cash. The charge is added to your account. A "Cosmo Planet" robot welcomes you at the door. You might expect the speech but not the change in facial expression as the robot greets each shopper. This robot was the official mascot of Expo 85 held in Tsukuba.

Prices for each item are clearly shown by light-emitting diode displays. They are updated daily by the central computer. As the shopper's hand reaches for an item, an infrared sensor detects the hand and gives a recorded description of the item being selected. Roving robots announce specials and new products. A recipe-information system can do an 850-item search at the request of the family cook. Nutrition evaluation services and household programming services are imminent.

The meat section is the high-tech star of the store. The shopper views, from the outside, a robot-operated, self-enclosed, sanitary environment. After selecting the cut of meat, the thickness, and the number of slices, the shopper is shown the price and can then accept or reject the order. If satisfactory, the order is sliced, weighed, wrapped, and priced. Meanwhile a female voice explains everything in the thirty to forty-five seconds taken by the whole process.

Behind the scenes a computer handles all the requirements for a store that receives 6,000 customers each day: lighting, air conditioning, freezers, and sterile kitchens. More than 150 sensors handle security, disaster warnings, and other systems, while a spray-mist system sterilizes the food-processing area.

Never happen here, you say? If you think not, you're probably one of those people who believed that blacksmiths, steam engineers and milkmen had job security. What about the argument that people will always want the personal touch, and that automation is too impersonal? At Seiyu, one store executive told me that sales at this store are well above those at their non-robotized outlets, partly because clerks can now really provide personal attention to the customer.

→   *Marine Ranching*

During the construction of the 1985 world exposition at Tsukuba, Japan, I watched workmen erect the first *himawari* (designed by Kei Mori). During a later trip to Japan, I saw it work. The *himawari* helped one ordinary – not genetically altered – tomato seed turn into a "tree" fifteen feet high and thirty feet across that produced fifteen thousand tomatoes during a six-month period. This giant tomato plant was inside, in the shade!

Dr. Mori has not taken early retirement. He has opened his *himawari* – Japanese for sunflower – to new worlds. Not content with bringing a new, ultraviolet-free form of healthful sunshine to

165

house and building interiors, Dr. Mori has now embarked on one of the most revolutionary concepts to come out of Japan: to move the sun to the bottom of the sea.

As mentioned, the *himawari* is a cluster of Fresnel lenses about seven feet wide, enclosed in an acrylic ball, and sitting on a rotating frame that tracks the sun. This surrounding ball filters out the majority of harmful ultraviolet rays from the sun. The "pure" sunlight is concentrated through the lens and directed, via fiber-optic cables, to an interior, darkened area where the sunlight is released (Dr. Mori speaks of "value-added solar rays"). This can be a residence, an office tower, an industrial plant, a hothouse, or a mine. No longer is this experimental: 146 patents have been approved and another 322 are pending. There are now more than fifty completed installations worldwide, the majority in Japan.

The most recent conceptual jump was the idea of carrying this sunlight to the ocean floor. Dr. Mori recently presented this concept at the first annual meeting of the Japan Institute for Macro-engineering. He outlined his idea for a "marine ranch." It would even be viable under the floating cities now being considered for the ocean off Japan.

On the piers anchoring such a floating city (at least thirty feet below the surface and above the seabed), observation corridors would be arranged in a honeycomb pattern. Photosynthetic chlorella culture tanks would hang from the corridors. With sunlight directed through fiber-optic cables from Mori's "optical radiator" onto these tanks, food would grow rapidly as the tanks are continually fed nutrients from the rich lower stratum of the sea. As part of this process, the ocean-ranch system would alleviate the stratification problem that affects all large bodies of water, especially in the summer.

At an optimum time the tanks would be discharged, pouring the mature chlorella algae into the surrounding area for the benefit of the lower levels of the food chain. With the increasing abundance of such food, higher levels of the aquatic food chain would also proliferate. First smaller, then larger fish would be attracted to the area, thus naturally restocking the sea. A more important though subtle effect is that a natural cleansing system would be created. By recycling bottom waste into higher forms of organic material, the ocean-ranch would purify the water.

The Japanese have also made great strides in raising salmon. In the late 1980s, they announced that they had raised the king (coho) salmon for the first time in captivity. Years ago they had tried the same experiments with devastating results – half the fish died. They have finally succeeded by thinking differently and using unconventional methods.

Salmon breed in fresh water, spawn upriver, and then die. When hatched, the fry spend about a year in their freshwater habitat and then return to the sea for their growth cycle, which varies depending on species. In North America, we usually catch them as they return to spawn. We use expensive netting techniques and lots of gasoline. It isn't cost efficient, and it depletes available resources.

The Japanese tried keeping the fry in fresh water for shorter periods of time. That didn't work. Then they tried longer periods. Finally they hit upon the secret. If you keep salmon in fresh water for two years, they don't grow any larger than they did after one year, but they develop into "superfish." They swim faster and are more successful in competing for natural food.

So the Japanese released these fry into fenced-off areas called "crawls" – salt water fjords, in effect. In just six months these fish experienced an average weight gain of 600 percent, from ten ounces to almost four pounds. It was unheard of. And their food was natural because of tidal flow through the barrier nets. The operators could check on them for disease with minimum effort. The free-swimming area was large enough to prevent seabed fouling. The grown salmon were easily harvested without damage. These higher quality fish were processed nearby immediately. Compare this to the standard technique of putting them in the ship's hold, packed with ice, to travel for two to ten days before processing.

This is not good news for the North American salmon fishery, and Japan's innovations do not stop there. The Japanese recently accomplished an even more remarkable feat by breeding lobsters in captivity.

9

Education

→ *Obsolescence in
the Schools*

For decades we have been hearing about all the leisure time we will
have in the new Communications Age. Perhaps the techno-peasants
will, but not those at the cutting edge. Why? Because people working
in the sunrise industries are finding that the rate of change requires
them to spend almost one day a week just to keep up with what's
new. This is especially true in computer companies, but also applies
in such fields as biotechnology and advanced medical services.

As you look into this phenomenon, it is easy to see why traditional
educational institutions cannot function in a new environment where
information travels at the speed of light. Never mind governments that
are still operating from manuals written in the 1930s and 1960s; let's
take teachers. In times of little change, it was easy to keep up with that
change. But as change accelerated, it changed the very environment
itself. Where once educators had 130 years to learn about, say, electricity

(after the invention of the electric motor, for example), today they have just weeks to learn what's new. The educational system isn't structured to handle rapid change. The students are aware of that.

Perhaps even more important is that those who do keep abreast of change just don't have the time to become teachers or even to train teachers. By the time that would occur in the old format, the thing they dropped out of in order to teach would itself be obsolete. Look at the speed at which we went from vacuum tubes to transistors to the microchip to integrated circuits to fifth generation artificial intelligence computers. Already biological and neural computers are pushing the frontiers of the sixth and seventh generation.

Knowledge is now really worthwhile only if it comes from the cutting edge. By the time it is passed on by an obsolete method, it is itself obsolete. Virtually anything passed on in print is outdated. Are you aware that it sometimes takes eight years to get a textbook into the educational pipeline in North America? The book is obsolete the day it is written, never mind the day it appears in the classroom, yet we're supposedly training kids for the future with this material.

Many universities are not aware of the speed at which knowledge is expanding. The mission statement of the president of the University of British Columbia, titled "Toward the Pacific Century: The President's Report," published in 1988, stated that knowledge was doubling every fifteen years (without citing a reference). A few years after the UBC report, the prestigious *Futurist* magazine reported that human knowledge was doubling every twenty months.

North American schools simply aren't aware of what is happening. Of course, there are minute pockets of awareness, but they are minimal, and educators with an eye on the future have little opportunity to be heard in the rigid higher levels of academia, where the rulers usually are not willing to give up their cherished beliefs in the long-gone educational dogma of yesterday. Hence, my view that the present educational system will not evolve but collapse.

Only those who learn to dance with electrons will thrive. Many others will not even survive. Would you be at your present level of influence and affluence today if you could not read or write? You needed to know the three Rs of the Industrial Age – reading, 'riting, and 'rithmetic – to survive. Today, if you have not acquired the knowledge of the new three Rs – RAM, ROM, and run – you are electronically illiterate. Our schools, instead of preparing students for the future, imprison them in the past.

→ *Does Literacy Matter?*

Back in 1989, *U.S. News & World Report* was calling for action against "The Illiteracy Epidemic." There are twenty-five million Americans who cannot read or write. Another forty-five million are functionally illiterate. More than 25 percent of the population is not equipped mentally to handle the Industrial Age, never mind the Information Age. In Canada the figures may be slightly better but the problem remains.

Criteria for literacy change with the times. One hundred years ago, as the Agricultural Age was winding down, the ability to merely write your own name put you in the "literate" class. Fifty years later, as the Industrial Age came into full flower, a sixth-grade education provided the same status. Today the bare minimum for Information-Age entry requires reading and writing skills at the level of a high school graduate. The trouble now is that students are graduating from high school unable to read and write adequately.

To compete and to maintain present levels of influence and affluence, North Americans must come up with innovative methods to update those among the population who are woefully behind and to carry the entire population to higher levels of knowledge. The alternative? Have you ever witnessed rural peasants grubbing out a living from the dry desert soil in the mountains of Mexico and Peru? Their ancestors were the Aztecs and the Incas, rulers of advanced civilizations and lords of all their known world.

Education is the crucial factor. As Mortimer B. Zuckerman, editor-in-chief of *U.S. News & World Report*, correctly points out, "In the post-industrial era, when the majority of people in the work force make a living with their minds, not their hands, it is education – more than coal or steel or even capital – that is the key to our economic future."

In Japan, IQs of over 130 are recorded among 10 percent of the high school population. Literacy there has reached new heights, and instant communications and utilization of information have become commonplace. With a relatively homogeneous native population, and citizens who speak only one language in their homeland (unlike Canada or the U.S.), the Japanese are capable of communications that are faster and more comprehensive.

Yet it is not time for total despair. Illiteracy has its advantages. I have found that the best young programmers are kids who can't spell. They naturally spell phonetically, as robots do. What was once a liability becomes an asset in another age.

Literacy is bound to become less important in years to come. For some time now, I have had what looks like a hippie headband that picks up my alpha and beta waves. Using biofeedback, I can turn on my computer, tell it to run a program, and command my computer to print. Today a wire runs from the headband to the computer and its peripherals. Tomorrow that wire will not be necessary.

My satellite dishes have a device known as a Low-Noise Amplifier or LNA, which takes the very faint signal (quieter than a snowflake falling) from outer space and amplifies it up to 200,000 times. I get all the color, pictures, and sound required. Imagine a modification of such a device, perhaps the size of a hearing aid, that could amplify your thought waves. It might have to amplify your thought waves two or three million times, but then you could create miracles on command. You could instruct a bulldozer to move mountains, right from your easy chair. No reading or writing necessary.

I suggest a different look at print illiteracy. Just because part of the population does not know how to read and write it doesn't mean those people will be unable to obtain knowledge levels that are viable for the twenty-first century.

→ *Teaching for Tomorrow*

I have on my desk a fat, forty-eight-page folder of courses published by a local school board on its continuing education program. It's great: more than one thousand courses, from crafts and cosmetic surgery to Tagalog, the language of the Philippines. These courses are offered during the day, in the evening, even on weekends. They make learning easy, and the student fees are low.

But is anyone teaching about tomorrow? Like most schools, this one teaches the known. Today's marketplace offers premiums to those who search out the unknown. This process requires a knowledge navigator, but our schools aren't producing any.

In an age where change is constant, where the most secure job can be wafted out of existence by the breeze of the next technological advance, our schools aren't teaching students how to adapt to rapid change. No earthling is capable of welding better than a robot, yet many schools still teach welding. With the electronic camera about to devastate professional photographers, they still teach photography. With ceramic materials replacing metal cutlery, they teach metallurgy. New knowledge and technological advances now move at the speed of light, yet our schools aren't even trying to develop the people who can survive and lead the way to tomorrow.

A recent letter from a gentleman in Calgary, Alberta, mentions that he stopped building office buildings just before the recession because he realized that, with corporate downsizing and advances in data storage, corporations wouldn't require more buildings. Yet no politician saw this coming, or believed anybody who had that vision. No government drew attention to the change (or wanted to stop the tax revenue). They all thought alike. This gentleman listened, watched, and then made his decision. He survived with his fortune intact, not because he had learned about the past but because he looked to the future.

Does your local school have a course in futurism? Does any teacher, school board member, or politician even begin to understand the possibilities and implications of the Communications Age? Ask around. Phone your local school board or teachers' union. You'll be shocked.

→   *Grads with*
         Warranties

Starting in 1994, the Los Angeles Unified School District – the second largest in the United States, with a student population of 640,000 – will send its graduates out into the world with a warranty, along with the usual diploma. The education warranty will work just like a car warranty. If the hired student's skills do not match those promised in the warranty, the school will absorb the cost of bringing that student up to the required level. The idea is also under consideration in Maryland and Massachusetts.

This innovation is not unexpected. For the past decade, business in both the United States and Canada has been telling the educational establishment that a mere high school diploma no longer carries the same value as in the past. *Time* magazine reported that Pacific Bell complained that "more than half of its applicants for entry-level jobs, such as operators, fail a simple seventh-grade reading and math test. Many others companies have reported similar experiences." A large number of Canadian business operations have been making similar complaints for some time.

The Los Angeles warranty covers more than basic reading, mathematics, and effective communications. Students must also have adequate thinking skills. They must be able to solve problems, reason logically, and describe mental visualizations. They must possess such personal qualities as integrity, self-management, initiative, and re-

174

sponsibility. These graduates will be expected to know how to budget time and resources such as money, materials, and staff. They must know, not learn on the job, how to lead, negotiate, and work on a team. They must know how to use technology to access, organize, and interpret data, how to understand and improve social and organizational systems, and they must be able to select and apply trouble-shooting technology. If they don't, the employer can bounce them back. And if they don't measure up when they return, as with a car, you stop dealing with that school and its product.

Gabriel Cortina, assistant superintendent on the Labor Secretary's Commission on Achieving Necessary Skills (SCANS), doesn't beat around the bush. "In the business world, sharing responsibility for a project is called teamwork. In classrooms, the way we teach today, it's called cheating." Many business executives say the warranty is needed and that the educational establishment in Los Angeles has finally been willing to confront a serious problem. It will be fascinating to see how well the program works, and whether other jurisdictions in the U.S. and Canada follow suit.

→   *Third World*
        Leapfrog

These words of British-born Arthur C. Clarke, the twentieth century's leading living visionary, appear on a sign in Sri Lanka: "2,000 years ago, Sri Lanka was one of the most technologically advanced countries in the world." Today it's a Third World country with fifteen million citizens. Does that mean it's doomed to spend the next 2,000 years as a have-not and know-not country? Not if Clarke has his way.

These days Clarke is helping the country make some bold attempts to leapfrog Industrial Age mentality. The author of *2001: A Space Odyssey*, and more than forty other publications, is aiding this renaissance on the tiny Indian Ocean island of which he is a long-time resident. Just outside Colombo, the capital, he spear-headed the construction of the Arthur C. Clarke Institute for Modern Technologies by donating the prize money from his presti-gious Marconi Award to the school. With the government's help, he hopes that this institution will grow into a leading center for Third World development of new technologies.

Ironically, the lack of what were previously called Industrial Age advantages now appear to be a benefit to such countries. With no big financial investment in old-world technologies and with no huge educational bureaucracy in the way, change can happen quickly. Not blinded by the defective vision of the status quo, Sri Lankans may have found the better way to go.

India is in a similar position. With a population closing in on a billion and a Third World economy, India does not have the funds to provide the books and computers, never mind the school buildings and staff, to give its burgeoning population a survival learning system of the old-fashioned sort. Like Sri Lanka, however, India is thinking smarter. The government is sending out TV sets to the 750,000 villages in the country. There the "head man" sets up an open-air shelter for the TV set. A small low-cost satellite dish brings in the signal. In most cases, the village doesn't have the electricity to power the set, so a bicycle with a generator accompanies each TV. The local contest is to see which kid can peddle the longest supplying power, before the screen starts to flicker. Overnight, people who have never seen a video image leave behind the old ways and enter the new.

That's what I call public education.

→   *Technology and
        Education*

In our globalizing world, emerging technologies have done wonders for productivity in manufacturing, medicine, biotechnology, and engineering, to mention just a few of the many sectors affected. Yet schools, among the most conservative of institutions, have generally failed to embrace these changes. New jobs are waiting for trained workers in some industries, but our schools are not training them. Some industries have set up their own training schools because public school graduates simply aren't aware of what those industries are all about.

The problem is serious, and can only become more so. The increasing rate of change in new technology means that schools will have more and more difficulty keeping up. *Technology In Education: Looking Toward 2020* (edited by Raymond S. Nickerson and Philip P. Zodhiate), though a very good book on this subject, was in some ways obsolete by the time it reached wide distribution.

Changes in information storage alone have moved from advanced microfiche, where a printed newspaper page was reduced to fingernail size, to optical storage cards the size of a credit card that hold twenty thousand pages of information. Within three years of that advance both Grolier and Britannica announced that their respective twenty-one and twenty-nine volume encyclopedia sets were available on 4.5-inch compact disks. Tufts University followed with a crystal the size of a sugar cube that held the information equivalent of ten thousand one-megabyte floppy disks, only to be outclassed by Cambridge University, which put the whole *Encyclopedia Britannica* on the head of a pin. Since the announcement of that old-fashioned development, SERODS have appeared on the scene. A major library can now be held in your hand.

This is just one field. Such change is occurring everywhere. As mentioned, when Digital Equipment Corporation of Maryland built the VAX 780 minicomputer, it was three feet high, three feet wide, and six feet long. It cost $30,000 to manufacture. Six years later the same company came out with a microchip the size of a fingernail that cost $300 to make. It replaced the VAX 780. The highly skilled, highly paid workers who produced and serviced the VAX 780 were no longer required. Change, like death, can come on swift wings.

The old ways, the expensive ways, no longer work. They must be replaced by dramatic changes in our thinking. Such changes are happening elsewhere on the planet. The more forward-thinking peoples are no smarter than we are, but they have realized that nothing will ever again be like it was in the past. In many cases people in the emerging countries in Asia didn't have any "good old days" to look back on, so it was easier for them to adapt. In North America, meanwhile, trying to hang on, trying to pressure governments to support long-dead concepts in manufacturing, services, education, or even government itself, is a waste of effort, money, and time.

Chester Finn, a Vanderbilt University professor, comments, "There are only two major institutions in America today where, if you walk into them, you would feel like you could be there a century ago. They are schools and churches."

I think he's right. The public education system should be preparing us for the next century, not keeping us mired in the past. The possibilities are greater than our teachers have been trained to comprehend. How will we compete with countries that have seen the future and are prepared to enhance it?

→ *Can Johnny Spell?*

Are you old enough to remember when automatic turn indicators were not permitted on cars? How about when ballpoint pens were not allowed in schools? Eighty years ago you weren't even allowed to take an automobile into the province of Prince Edward Island!

Remember the days, more recently, when kids couldn't take hand-held calculators into school? They were forced to use paper and pencil – because it had always been done that way. Some schools still prohibit kids from taking their own laptop computers into classrooms. What if the kids came up with the answer more quickly than the teacher?

Teachers and parents often bemoan the fact that Johnny can't spell, and the computer is often blamed. The fact is, though, wasting weeks and months learning how to spell may not be productive. In the Communications Age it may be more profitable to spend that time learning how to think.

In that case, how will kids ever know how to spell? A California software company, Working Software Inc., already has a range of programs that include "Lookup," which instantly finds the correct spelling for any word. The two dictionaries built into this program contain 93,000 and 60,000 words. Using this program is much faster than reaching for a Gutenberg-style dictionary. The program contains a "guess" function, which makes guesses based on phonetic spelling. It also catches common typos and uses a wild-card method to locate all words beginning and ending with certain specified letters. For example, if you entered "comm?er", it would find all words beginning with "comm" and ending with "er."

Two other programs from Working Software contain a legal dictionary and a medical dictionary. Still another program in the same family, "Findswell," will find anything you have placed in your computer's memory. Try that with your own head!

This isn't the only example of why we may not need to teach kids how to spell. When robots are programmed to speak, they are "taught" to use phonetic spelling. They spell a word the way it sounds, just like humans often do when they misspell a word. Robots love that intelligent method. Take the word "laugh": if you were an intelligent robot, wouldn't you see right away that "laf" is the way to go? Humans, with their correct spelling, may soon find their knowledge a handicap in dealing with robots – or the future.

The new race of neutral computers will not seek perfection (in spelling or anything else) at a high price in time and cost, but it will find the "almost perfect" answer almost instantly and practically for free. Perhaps we ought to be taking the same approach in our classrooms.

→   *The Whittle*
     Phenomenon

Since 1989, Whittle Communications of Knoxville, Tennessee, has been installing *free* equipment to bring satellite transmissions to American classrooms. Whittle has taken the reins and is turning the educational establishment around. Its program, Channel One, is a daily twelve-minute news, geography, and information program designed to make the world relevant to teenagers. It is the only daily newscast produced exclusively for secondary school students. Channel One is beamed via satellite to participating schools every day of the school year. There is no cost to the school. Two of the daily twelve minutes of programming is advertising. If a school guarantees to broadcast at least nine out of ten shows to the students, it gets free satellite dishes, free VCRs, free TVs, and the free programming.

Starting with a six-school test program in March 1989, Channel One had expanded by the end of 1990 to 6,000 schools. Within seventy-five days, there were 8,216 schools in forty-seven states being set up to receive programs – 615 in one week. Today more than 10,000 schools, 300,000 classrooms, and 6.1 million students are getting education from the medium they've grown up with. It's not just passive entertainment. In September 1991, the state of Michigan and the Whittle Educational Network held a live video-teleconference to help 10,000 mathematics teachers prepare for a statewide exam – the largest number of schools (515) ever to participate in such an endeavor.

Created by Christopher Whittle in 1970, Whittle Communications now has 1,200 employees and does more than $200 million a year in business. It produces magazines and wall media (e.g., posters). It has twelve information centers, two book series, and three television systems. Whittle is on the way up. It's providing what the market wants, not pushing the old mush down students' throats in an antiquated system. Time-Warner Inc., the media giant with deep pockets, is a 50 percent owner; there's no capital shortage here. It's not available in Canada because of Canadian telecommunications regulations.

Whittle points out that "when Edison invented electric illumination, he didn't tinker with candles to make them burn better. Instead, he created something brilliantly new: the light bulb." Whittle Communications is lighting the way along a new educational path. It will be starting a new nationwide school system, offering contract services for public and private schools, and developing educational software, hardware, and the infrastructure (satellite dishes, VCRs, TVs) along with an educational-research laboratory already under way.

By 1996, the company envisages having up to two hundred campuses with 150,000 students age one to six, and perhaps a thousand schools and two million students by the turn of the century. It will spend $60 million to get this Edison Project going and $2.5 billion for the one hundred to two hundred campuses planned for 1996. It does not intend to compete for government grants.

Whittle hired Benno Schmidt, then president of Yale University, to be president and chief executive officer of the Edison Project. Why would he accept such a post? "The schools of America are in difficulty and need fundamental structural change," he says, "not tinkering around the edges." Hear, hear!

→ The Ultimate
School

We have all learned a lot from our cars. Most of what we learned came not from the car itself, but from our using it to get to places we hadn't been before. We have driven to mountain tops, beside rivers, along coastal plains, through city streets, and under bridges. All that data stored in our craniums thanks to our travels gave us insight and perspective and something we didn't have before – the ability to think differently.

People flying airplanes, helicopters, and space shuttles have acquired additional data, perspective, and insight. When we see something from a height, we see it differently and think about it differently. Spend some time in a submarine and watch how quickly new thinking patterns emerge. Every exploratory experience encourages a change in thinking.

What about education? We are still pushing the old three *R*s, even though the parents of today's school children are already receiving 70 percent of *their* information from television. Schooling is supposed to prepare us for handling the world we will enter. But that world has changed faster than teachers can be trained. In many cases today, such as computer operation, television, and pattern recognition, the kids are more expert than their teachers. Shouldn't this tell us something?

A cyberspace exploratory world – one in which piezoelectric vibro-tactile actuators respond to every feeling possible in the "real" world – will allow us to learn at a speed and a level never before possible. Consider a stove. Adults know a stove is hot, probably because they once got burned. In a cybernetic world of virtual reality, you don't have to go through the pain to understand. You experience the burn, the heat, and even the pain – but without the damage.

How many kids have stuck their fingers in a light socket? A great thrill if you live to tell about it. Now you can. In a virtual room with a virtual light socket, you will receive the same apparent shock, but it won't kill you. Your mind will indelibly imprint that experience so you'll know better in the future.

We all did the dissect-the-frog-in-biology-class bit. It's not popular anymore because of enhanced sensibilities and the environment movement. But why not dissect a virtual frog in a virtual laboratory? That's painless learning for all, including the frog. Many kids find history a bore. It won't be, if you're high in the rigging of a pirate ship about to rape and plunder Kingston, Jamaica, or in Parliament hearing Disraeli speak, or in Philadelphia listening to Ben Franklin describe his electrical experiment with a kite.

All this is now possible to a limited extent. Soon it will be much more realistic. When virtual reality merges with holographic projection (not unlike the marriage of television to the VCR), stand back! The world will change faster than it has during any previous technological advance. It will be the biggest thing in education since the alphabet. Cyberspace will become the ultimate school. The sooner the educational establishment wakes up to the possibilities, the better equipped our young people will be for the world that awaits them.

→   *Nintendo Learning*

"I think the school is an extremely harmful institution. . . . I think the schools do more harm than Nintendo." These are the words of Seymour A. Papert, considered by some to be the world's leading expert on the use of computers in education. He's with the renowned Media Laboratory at the Massachusetts Institute of Technology.

Why do students leave school? Mostly because of boredom. Yet Nintendo can hold a kid's interest for hours. Maybe we are doing something wrong. Papert believes the key question is: What makes some people become so passionately interested in something? He invented the computer programming language Logo and has recently received a research grant from Nintendo. He told the *Toronto Star* that he "has made no promises to Nintendo, although he does not rule out the possibility of developing educational software for its game machines." He adds that schools have failed to stay up-to-date in adapting new technologies to the classroom. His new goal: to make such classroom subjects as writing and history as alluring to children as Teenage Mutant Ninja Turtles or Super Mario Brothers.

For the past five years, someone else has been asking similar questions. He's not a professor, but a successful businessman. Jack Taub is founder of the world's first information utility, The Source, which he sold for megabucks to Reader's Digest. He is now founder and chairman of the International Education and Information

Utility. He believes his creation will make a child, when given the option of going to a theme park or delving into his magical computer world of knowledge, choose the computer. Let's hope he's right.

Meanwhile, the disinterest in public education is staggering. In British Columbia, the drop-out figures are almost unbelievable: out of 476,000 students, 38 percent drop out before they enter high school; and 78 percent of those who start high school drop out before entering college. Of those who enter college, 75 percent drop out before receiving a degree.

The Globe and Mail reported that even the Toronto Board of Education has finally realized something is up. The board is now "quizzing students to see why they have turned their backs on traditional classrooms." Students said things like, "[School] buildings . . . [imply] that students are animals and can't be trusted to respect public property," and "Student Council is really just the dance committee" and has no power. Others felt that they were "always going to assemblies" (echoing office workers who complain that they're always going to meetings).

If you think it has to do with money, you're wrong. Canada spends twice per capita on education as Japan does. The 1990 U.S. State Education Performance Chart shows graduation rates still dropping and performance on college entrance exams still falling, although spending on education is increasing – 21 percent after inflation last year.

Can people like Papert and Taub revive our young people's interest in public education? They've got the right idea and the right attitude. Technology will play as important a role in the classroom as it already plays in the world at large.

→ *Classroom Innovations*

When was the last time you got any real understanding of a child's progress in school from reading a traditional report card? Did it show what he or she was learning? Could it express his or her enthusiasm, or lack of it? Did it show the way he or she approaches a problem? What did it reveal about the school itself?

The parents of students at a class at San Diego State University in California now get grades and what lies behind them on their home television from videocassette report cards. Ninety-five percent of the parents receiving the modern video report cards approved of their use. Now the parents can really see how well, or otherwise, their offspring are performing. Students have to request the video critiques and provide blank tapes. Currently the tapes run about thirty to forty minutes. They include classroom activities, perhaps showing the student doing work or discussing something, as well as evaluations of his or her performance and work habits.

Not all educators think it's a great idea. Glen Broom, acting chairman at the same university's journalism department, is not a fan. He claims that it takes too much time to prepare such a report: "You would not have time to do your job." Broom also objects to sending video reports to parents. "We are dealing with students here," he states. "My client is the student, not the student's parents." If students volunteer and participate, however, how can that be an invasion of privacy?

According to Professor Donald Sneed, who heads the class, the new method outshines the old. "The standard university report card today is a computer printout, a piece of paper that only says A, B, C, D, or F," he explains. "There is no elaboration on why the grade was assigned. On videotape, you can provide much more information. You can even zoom in on papers to provide specific examples of a student's work." Probably the greatest indirect benefit is what students learn about communications skills while helping to develop their own video report cards.

Another classroom innovation is the copyboard, first developed by Okidata. The copyboard is a large white board, much like the old-fashioned blackboard, easily wheeled into class. It comes in two sizes. The large model is roughly three feet by four feet; the smaller model is three by two. The teacher or instructor uses special markers in blue, black, green, or red and writes directly on the board.

Don't bother taking notes. Pay attention and listen. Chemical reactions, complicated medical information, football plays, schematic diagrams for engineers or architects – the copyboard remembers them all. When the speaker is finished, he counts the students in class, hits a button, and out come clean copies of whatever was written on the copyboard. And like an old-fashioned blackboard, it wipes clean with an eraser.

→　　*Parlez-Vous?*

According to Charles Berlitz, who should know, there are 2,796 languages spoken on this planet. Governments, especially in Canada, have spent countless millions on language training in the schools. But is language training necessary in the Communications Age? Could we be putting that time and money to better use in preparing our young people for the world that awaits them?

In British Columbia, where I live, it costs $7,000 a year to put a student through high school, which works out to about six dollars per student per hour. The cost is about $800 per month (including teachers' salaries, school overhead, etc.) for a student to get twenty hours of language instruction.

There is a better way. Arthur Wright, from Inglewood, Australia, suggests that, if students want to learn Spanish, for example, we send them to Guatemala. There, for about $400 each a month, they would get room and board with a local family; six hours of tuition a day and up to another ten hours a day with Spanish-speaking hosts; one teacher per student.

Do these kids sit in a dull classroom listening to a non-Spanish teacher? No. Their teacher/guide takes them around town, visiting shops, libraries, restaurants, and so forth. They learn the way the language is really spoken. They learn it quickly because their environment forces them to. After one month of this total immersion, students usually speak Spanish more fluently than students who have attended North American public education language classes for five or six years.

If we want students to learn a second language, there's a better way. But are second and third languages going to be needed in the future? Fujitsu, Japan's largest computer company, has developed the "universal translator." It can translate Japanese into English and vice versa at the rate of one thousand words per minute. It can translate half a dozen languages simultaneously. The blind can hear the program and the deaf can read it. A printout is available if you so desire, in the language of your choice. Will people want to learn another language when there is no longer any economic incentive to do so – when a machine can efficiently translate for you?

The major Japanese telephone service (NTT) recently announced that it will offer an automatic translation service by 1995. You will phone Japan and speak the language of your choice. People on the other end will hear only Japanese. They will reply in their native tongue, but you will hear English, French, Italian, German – whatever language you prefer.

For skeptics, I sometimes show at my seminars a videotape from a satellite transmission showing a Kenyan broadcasting from Japan to a Canadian in Iqaluit, Northwest Territories. The Kenyan is speaking Swahili. The Canadian is speaking Inuktitut. Because the translation is digitized and synthesized, one person could have been blind and the other deaf, and they still would have understood each other! Such advances in technology suggest that the money we spend on language training could possibly be put to better use.

10

What Else Is New?

→ *The Wisdom Machine*

Everyone's heard the term *artificial intelligence*, but few are aware of the drama unfolding in this rapidly advancing field. About ten years ago the Japanese announced plans to create a fifth-generation artificial intelligence computer to surpass anything known at that time. The project has since created new concepts and new hardware – along with consternation, competition, and concern. Politicians, computer scientists, and industry leaders in North America and Europe feared that the Japanese would capture both an intellectual and industrial lead that would, for the next century, put them ahead of western countries.

For this project, "knowledge engineers" have been gathering information for expert systems. Reports say Japan now has two hundred knowledge engineers, and wants twenty thousand. A knowledge engineer practically lives with an expert for six months or so. The engineer feeds into the fifth-generation computer all books, tests, examinations, etc. that the expert has read or compiled in a lifetime. If the expert is a medical doctor, all the medical training is fed in, including diagnoses, patient histories, prognoses, and other relevant information. Patient histories do not include the names, but do include age, geographic locations, and other pertinent data. This includes data that we in the West might not consider, but which some Japanese think is important, such as children's growth as a function of the color and ceiling height of the rooms in which they live.

By the end of the six months, a great deal of information is in the computer. Discussions and diagnoses (with follow-ups) of all patients that the physician interviews during that period are also fed in. The computer, in effect, knows what the doctor knows: the doctor's intuition, observations, and medical facts. It does not stop there. The same procedure will take place a thousand times; the computer will eventually have all the known intelligence of one thousand physicians in its data bank. This will be made available to all Japanese hospitals. With a difficult case, hospital personnel can tap this fifth-generation computer and use its knowledge to interpret symptoms under study at some distant hospital.

It is not only in medicine that the intelligence of these experts is being mined. There is similar information being obtained from engineers, physicists, chemists, anthropologists, botanists, and so on. When the project is completed, "the wisdom machine" theoretically will be able to give an advanced and knowledgeable response to any question asked. Problems that today seem intractable will be approached in new and innovative ways by the fifth-generation intelligence machine. Its answers will be available in any language. The machine can already translate Japanese into English and vice versa at the rate of one thousand words a minute in voice or print.

→ *The New Paper*

Paper first appeared in 3500 B.C. in the form of papyrus. It was a boon to written communications right up to the fifteenth century. Then when Gutenberg developed his printing press, the paper explosion really took off. Today paper is everywhere. Its use has even grown in the early years of the computer age. But for how long?

For more than a hundred years now Canada has provided a good living for many of its citizens from the wealth produced by paper made from trees grown in its forests. Today pulp mills are working increasingly longer shifts, the price of pulp is rising, and labor unions are demanding ever increasing salaries. Now technology offers a new threat.

The name is kenaf (pronounced ka-naf). It's a tropical Asian plant of the hibiscus family. It looks similar to sugar cane or bamboo, grows in the same climates, and can be cultivated with many of the same growing techniques and equipment as cane or bamboo. It could, along with the now genetically altered loblolly pine (formerly known as "the weed of the forest"), provide devastating competition to present sources of pulp from the forests of the Pacific Northwest and indeed from any temperate zone woodlot.

Most trees take from seven to forty years to reach a usable size for pulp. Just making paper requires vast amounts of water and energy; in addition, roughly 10 percent of the wood cut is wasted. Paper is also rapidly depleting the numbers of oxygen-providing trees. The pulp-making process uses acid or alkali, depending on the class of pulp desired, to break down the fibers. That material pollutes rivers and streams, causing wide-ranging problems. Trees in Canada usually number about 100 to the acre. Loblolly pine is now growing in sandy soil in the southern states at 250 trees to the acre. With the loblolly pine, enzymes instead of sulfites break down the fibers. After the process is completed, that water goes back into the streams too, but it is totally biodegradable.

Kenaf is another magnitude ahead of this. It can produce 300 to 500 percent more pulp per acre per year than trees – at half the cost. In four to five months it becomes high-quality newsprint paper. Such paper takes longer to fade, requires less ink, and provides higher contrast. Waste in kenaf production is double that of normal trees, but the relative total cost of the waste is minimal because kenaf is so cheap to produce.

Kenaf is already being planted in quantity in Mexico and southern Texas. In Thailand recent estimates say it is already providing 10 percent of the country's newspaper requirements. Look for a new kenaf plant to appear shortly near McAllen, Texas. It will be built by Kenaf International and is scheduled to produce 230,000 tons of newsprint per year. That alone would be one percent of the total U.S. paper production. Additional production is planned in another kenaf newsprint plant to be built by the Institut de Recherche in France.

With new environmental regulations coming into effect in 1994 in California, temperate forests that have been supplying a major portion of the world's newsprint will be in even deeper trouble. The new laws will not permit a newspaper to be sold in California unless it is at least 42 percent recycled fiber. Paper mills in Canada or even in the U.S. Pacific Northwest will no longer gather used papers in Los Angeles or New York or any other major North American city and truck those papers back to their present pulp or paper mills. It just won't be economically viable. It will, however, pay a Mexican company to send a barge to Los Angeles, gather up old newspapers, and take them back to Mexico, where they can be mixed with virgin kenaf to produce a superior, less expensive product.

Newsprint isn't the only thing you can make from kenaf. It also makes good carpet backing and molded auto parts. Canada's economy will feel its effects, but the country won't be producing kenaf of its own. It only grows in tropical or semi-tropical climates.

→   *Carbon Fiber*

Stronger, lighter high-rise towers are being built using less reinforced steel, along with carbon fiber, a product that could replace cancer-causing asbestos. First to gamble on incorporating carbon fiber into reinforced cement were the architects and builders of the 150-foot-high onion-shaped domes of the Saddam Qadassiya Martyrs monument built in Baghdad in 1983. The showcase thirty-seven-story Ark Hills office tower in Tokyo is the latest display of the advantages of this unique material.

Carbon that can be spun into a fiber is the result of heating a pulp-waste product called lignin. Discovered and patented by Thomas Edison for use in incandescent electric lamp filaments, carbon fiber was again patented eighty years later by Union Carbide for use as a reinforcing material. In 1963, Dr. Sugio Otani of Gunma University (northwest of Tokyo) became excited by it as a result of another project. He patented a process for commercial-scale plants to transform pitch into carbon fiber.

Most promising new applications for fiber involve use in reinforcing cement. Kajima, the giant Japanese construction company, has been working with Otani to create a cement mixture using only 3 percent chopped fiber. It is claimed that building walls with this material are stronger by a factor of three to four and are up to 60 percent lighter than anything constructed with traditional cement.

The Ark Hills office complex has 170 tons of carbon fiber incorporated into exterior curtain walls. Despite costs three times higher than ordinary cement, the new mixture nets out cheaper because it uses 20 percent fewer steel reinforcing rods and does not require heavy, expensive cranes to swing the lighter panels into place.

As land becomes increasingly expensive in Japan, many new buildings are being erected on reclaimed land. This land is usually softer, so lighter-weight buildings reduce the chance of subsidence.

Ten more buildings incorporating carbon fiber have been commenced in Japan since the Ark Hills project was designed. Several more buildings are planned for the near future.

Another new product is a long-lasting (fifty years) tile made from carbon-fiber cement, a modern roofing material produced in Europe in quantity. (Plant planning for U.S. manufacturing is already under way.) This tile was developed as a replacement for both the combustible wooden shingle and the carcinogenic asbestos-based shingle. The former has already been banned as a fire hazard in Los Angeles, and the latter is running into resistance everywhere from environmentally sensitive homeowners.

The carbon-fiber cement shingles are made in Switzerland with a slurry material that resembles pancake mix. Run through a roller press, the mixture produces large sheets that are dried and bonded in an autoclave. Cut, packaged, shipped, and applied like regular tiles, these carbon-fiber cement shingles are about half the cost of natural slate, with similar wear and fire-resistant characteristics. According to the Insurance Information Institute of California, some companies there give a discount for fireproof shingles and charge a higher premium for wooden shingles.

Although other uses for carbon fiber have been discovered, the big market would be as an asbestos replacement, although production costs must first be dramatically lowered. The Japanese government is restricting the sale of asbestos for health reasons (in the process putting eighty thousand workers in four hundred factories out of jobs).

Canadians, once well-liked everywhere as considerate, tolerant, responsible world citizens, now find that reputation at risk as their governments continue to push exports of asbestos to developing countries and promote the sale of combustible wooden shingles (yes, they are combustible even with fire retardants, for these reportedly evaporate within a decade, leaving the wooden shakes unprotected against fire).

→   *Metal Logs*

It looks as if another nail is being driven into the coffin of the Canadian forest industry. This time it's a Venezuelan company called Tronco with a product called Metalogs. That's right, metal logs that allow unskilled laborers to build what looks like a wooden log cabin in a quarter of the time required to erect the same-size building with logs or cut lumber from the forest. Also the material is 25 percent cheaper than wood. It doesn't burn and termites can't eat it.

This innovation is not limited to log cabins. Regular homes and two-story apartments or hotels can be constructed in the same fashion. Some recent Russian immigrants to Israel are now comfortably installed in a multi-unit apartment house completely built – from starting the foundation to moving in the new tenants – in six weeks!

How's it done? Picture a machine that forms steel tubes, accompanied by a generator and compressor, all together the size of a desk, which are loaded onto a small trailer that can be pulled up mountains or into the jungle, desert, or suburban lot by a small car or jeep. This is the "factory" for building a home, apartment, or warehouse. While some of the workers are pouring a slab foundation, the log machine arrives at the building site and goes to work. Rolls of strip steel or aluminum of varying small widths are fed into the machine. Instantly, out comes a "log" in the dimension and length required for a particular part of the building. This zero inventory procedure greatly minimizes the need for storage and transportation of building materials. When construction is completed at one site, the mobile production facility can be easily moved to the next.

When the foundation slab is dry, the logs are laid in horizontal fashion, just as in a wooden log house. However, putting these logs in place is much easier. They are light enough that two workers can easily handle the largest log and lift it into place. Smaller logs can provide the frames for the windows and doors, and these, along with widely spaced, thin metal studs screwed into all Metalogs, are installed vertically, giving additional structural support. The roof is made in the same fashion.

Electrical, fiber-optic computer, stereo, phone, or water lines can be run through the metal logs with ease. Other logs can serve as heating ducts or "sound corridors" for music. In mild climates thermal insulation is provided by the airspace within the logs. In colder climates the logs can be filled with fiberglass or other insulation for increased protection against cold or heat. Again, this is easily done with unskilled labor.

The home can be left with the log cabin appearance inside or outside, or it can be painted or sprayed with shockcrete, a form of concrete or stucco, and finished inside with gypsum board, wood paneling, or any kind of exotic finish the homeowner desires. When completed, the house can look like any other in the block.

Don't think these environmentally sound homes are flimsy. Building inspectors in Dade County, Florida, have found these unusual buildings strong enough to handle "killer" hurricanes. A patented hook-and-tie connector holds the logs firmly together at the corners to provide exceptional strength and stability. The system has been certified by major building codes in the United States. In Orlando, two large Tronco housing projects are under way, one a 354-unit apartment complex. In the well-to-do Coconut Grove district of Miami, Tronco houses even drew CNN and *Time* magazine to the scene to report on the "log cabin townhomes."

Now considered proven at home and in foreign test centers, this innovative building product is moving into other countries. In Venezuela there is now more than half a million square feet of space made with Metalogs, not only houses and apartments but also warehouses, schools, offices, and retail outlets.

The building industry, like any other, must stay keenly aware of what is happening around the world. In my seminars I tell corporate executives, "Set up your own Distant Early Warning line to spot technological changes that may wipe out your industry overnight.

Every corporation that wants to survive into the third millennium had better put someone on this project today. If not, the company stands a good chance of being out of business tomorrow."

→   *Bee Technology*

Seventeen years ago, when my houseboat home/office was under construction, a struggling company called International Structuralcomb in New Westminster, British Columbia, was producing what I thought was a product with a future – one that would reduce the number of trees required to build a house yet still provide exceptional strength and rigidity.

I had the Structuralcomb panels incorporated, where feasible, into my floating home, mainly for the floor of the second-story bedroom, which also became the kitchen ceiling. The panels were perfect. They absorb sound and insulate well. If I were building a home today I would use similar construction, perhaps complemented with Metalogs in some parts of the building.

Unfortunately, financial problems forced the company to quietly fold its panels. It was ahead of its time. Today a similar concept called Bellcomb Technologies is thriving in Minneapolis, Minnesota. This company is having more success. Why? Because a factor has come into play that wasn't considered important two decades ago – the environmental factor. Pressures against cutting wood, any kind of wood, are increasing. The "honeycomb" technology uses only seven cords of wood to construct a two-thousand-square-foot house instead of the twenty cords required by conventional construction.

To maintain a sustainable forest we are going to have to do "more with less," as Buckminster Fuller kept preaching for years – with few listeners. It is not enough to plant a tree or even two for each one cut. With a waste reduction of at least 75 percent, we are going to have to do a lot more with what we do cut. The Bellcomb process provides one practical path to follow.

Early developments along this line included the Mosquito Bomber, built from Douglas fir in a paper-and-wood honeycomb. It was great during wartime since bullets went right through aircraft covering, and patching afterwards was usually a simple glue or fabric job. Although the same principle was used in American Super Fortress Bombers, the idea never really caught on except as a widely used substitute for corrugated cardboard in the packaging industry.

In the 1970s the aerospace industry took another look. These companies started to use honeycomb in airplanes and spacecraft because, pound for pound, it is one of the strongest, most rigid products on earth. It has been used, for example, on John Glenn's space capsule, the interior structures for Skylab, and the shock-resisting hulls of the world's fastest hydroplanes. Military housing has used honeycomb since 1960.

An Australian engineer eventually came up with a process that made small volume, or short-run, manufacturing cost-effective. Today a custom-built home, office, or warehouse can be erected quickly with relatively unskilled labor. A Structuralcomb building was erected in twenty hours at the United Nations Habitat Conference in Vancouver by a team of fifteen unskilled women.

Construction of the honeycomb panels starts with a matrix of hexagons, following the honeybee's original plans. Two skins are added to make a stronger, absolutely flat panel. These skins may be paper, plastic, metal, wood veneer, cement, gypsum board, granite, or marble – almost anything as long as it is flat. Such beams can be tiny, or load-bearing, or adequate for three-story buildings.

Panels can be rendered water-resistant or fire-retardant, or, at extra cost, totally waterproof and fireproof. They can be designed to any specifications. Once you have the panels, only a glue gun and a screw gun are required to assemble the home. A honeycomb building costs considerably less than a traditional woodframe house, since it uses only two-thirds the wood, requires fewer workers, and has an uncomplicated construction. It may sound crazy, but technology at times can do amazing things. Just like the creatures that inspired it.

→   *Virtual Vision*

Ever throw something on the car dashboard and see the reflection in the windshield? Sometimes the reflection appears larger and out in front of the windshield, over the hood. This phenomenon is being turned into a new industry.

Private Eye is a device that tricks the eye into seeing something that isn't there. You wear a headband holding a tiny mono color video-screen about four inches in front of and to the right of your right eye. Your field of vision is only partly obstructed, allowing you to see outside the picture much as you would while watching a regular twelve-inch TV monitor. That's the purpose – to provide a nonexistent TV screen that appears to be located about two feet in front of you.

Since Private Eye is a monocular display and does not occupy the full field of vision, the background environment can be viewed independently or integrated with the display in the mind's eye. Thus the viewer can receive information from the display while operating other equipment or performing additional tasks. My assistant and I have been using that device for some time now in producing my electronic books. It allows the wearer, at least in this application, to watch two computer screens and handle two keyboards simultaneously. It does wonders for productivity. It is another Communications Age skill that one develops while learning to use these new toys.

There is another advance in this field, Virtual Vision Sport, which allows people to view large-screen TV images through sport sunglasses. The unit consists of video eyewear and a belt pack containing a TV tuner, a battery, and an interface system that connects to VCRs, camcorders, a satellite dish, or cable TV. The viewer perceives a big-screen TV image floating in space. This virtual image is generated by a video system in the eyewear, but it appears to be up to five feet in size diagonally and eight to fifteen feet in front of the viewer.

While not really a virtual reality product, it is a step in that direction. Consider the possibilities. Instead of paying top prices at a sports event, take an inexpensive seat in the top of the stadium and watch big screen color images through portable, five-ounce eyeglasses, while also watching the distant game below! You can even catch the instant replays. At home you can water the lawn while watching auto races or a movie. Anything broadcast, taped, picked up on your home satellite dish, or sent via your local cable channel can be easily switched to these glasses. Parents could even have a camcorder trained on a sleeping child while they talk with neighbors over coffee. The clear picture of the child is always within sight. It would appear as a double exposure or color overlay on the normal field of vision.

The Virtual Vision Sport also can be used as a color viewfinder for camcorders. By connecting the beltpack into the camcorder, the user can record tight shots while simultaneously seeing everything else in the surrounding area. The possibilities, both amateur and professional, are limited only by the imagination.

Imagine a mobile personal computer that will project a display screen, larger in size than a standard computer display, inside a pair of eyeglasses as information is entered on a laptop. The system will allow users to work in almost any environment, such as a bus, plane, or in an easy chair at home. Or picture a surgeon wearing such glasses and operating on a patient; without moving his or her head, the surgeon could glance at charts, monitors, and other readout information displayed inside the glasses. Security systems would work in a similar way without curtailing social life. Security guards would no longer be restricted to the video monitoring room.

People who are hearing impaired could use voice recognition software now available and use the eyewear to have talk translated into printed words and displayed inside the eyeglasses. A recent test of this process by WGBH, the pioneering Boston PBS station, had hearing impaired people sitting in a movie theater wearing the Virtual Vision Sport glasses. They were able to watch the movie and glance down and see the captions in the eyewear. It was a successful and emotional trial. One woman remarked tearfully that for the first time she could share movies with her family.

A twist on that technique will allow travelers to communicate with people who speak a different language. Using the same voice recognition software, the eyeglasses will translate any human language into printed words that will be displayed inside the eyeglasses for the user to read.

Guess who else has been testing these glasses? Muppet puppeteers. Now they can see the Muppets in action and at the same time keep their eyes on the puppets as they work above or below them. This is much more convenient than the traditional method of turning their heads to watch a TV monitor as they produce the show. Now the puppeteers can junk the monitor and see the puppets as an overlay or double exposure on the actual puppets they are operating. They can see what the audience will see instead of having to imagine it, or glimpsing a monitor they can only glance at briefly.

I'm already enjoying my virtual vision glasses.

→   *Light from Sludge?*

Sewer sludge, the bane of municipal engineers, has been building into a monumental problem over the years. In many cities it has become a real financial, administrative, and political headache.

How to deal with it? One technological advance that may accomplish the impossible will be given the ultimate field test in Houston, Texas. Houston hopes to get rid of its sewer sludge by pumping it into the ground – 4,500 feet into the ground. But it will not be left there. It will come back as a refined product – sterile ash – which looks like sand and can be used as aggregate for concrete or asphalt paving material. Even as ash it will have reduced the volume of solids in the sludge by about 95 percent. Picture a huge vertical pressure cooker running almost a mile underground. As the sludge material reaches the bottom, gravity and hydrostatic pressure create heat.

Temperatures rise to between 500° and 700°F. This heat in turn triggers chemical reactions that activate an oxidization process. That turns the chemicals and micro-organisms into a concentrated sterile ash. Continued pumping of new, raw, wet sewage sludge into the pressure cooker forces the now-harmless, inert, ashlike sludge-substance back to the surface. It might even be hot enough to heat water and generate electricity!

Houston will have the world's first commercially operated plant, but this is not the first try. The process has been used for smaller quantities of toxic wastes for about a century, but the cost for above-ground containers and the cost of energy to heat the process were more than a commercial operation could bear. Underground, such costs almost disappear.

The Oxidyne Corporation will build and operate the plant for the city of Houston. Their present operation has involved oven-drying their sludge into pellets and selling these to Florida for fertilizer. Now the federal Environmental Protection Agency (EPA) is about to stop that game by ruling the procedure illegal. The proposed regulations will affect existing landfill sites as improved capping and sealing systems will have to be implemented. All this adds to the costs of old-style dumping of such materials as sewage sludge.

In the Netherlands a company called Vertech has been operating a similar process, but near the surface, by adding oxygen. This company is planning a wet-oxidation process plant for the town of Apeldoorn. The Dutch, with the most intensive livestock-raising system in Europe, have tons of pig manure on hand. This has been recycled as fertilizer, but the smell never made the process a big seller and the fertilizer was regarded as a potential health hazard. Pathogens in the fertilizer could also infect pigs. Such pathogens are destroyed completely by the wet-oxidation process.

In Great Britain the Water Research Centre is investigating the process for England and other parts of Europe. Additional advantages to the process are that, unlike conventional methods, it gives off no emissions. Toxic and other hazardous wastes can be treated.

Heavy metals, it is believed, will be bound to the ash, but even if this proves not to be the case the savings in volume alone could extend landfill site volume by a factor of twenty.

→   *Harnessing*
        the Ocean

The question I am most often asked is: "What would you suggest my kids do to survive in the future?" My suggestion: get them into something you have never heard about before. Look for those fields that no school trains them for. Where do you find these "invisible" industries? There are hundreds. Let me describe just one.

Look at energy, but in a different way. Where does energy cost the most, in normal circumstances? Answer: on islands. If you can find a more efficient, lower-cost method than any known today to supply energy to islands, you would have a chance of replacing their existing sources of energy – and there are thousands of islands around the world.

Back in 1984 a Norwegian company, Kvaerner Brug, started researching such a possibility. About five years later it succeeded, and a coastal wave generator on the west coast of Norway began pumping electricity into Norway's national grid system. The company burned no oil or natural gas and used no coal; it used the energy from the waves. These units can be used at almost any shoreline location. The sea does not need to have huge waves or pounding surf, although those would produce even more power. The natural surge of the sea has huge power-generating potential, and it can now be harnessed.

As in all such research, fate sometimes steps in and reminds everyone of the risks inherent in any advance into the future. In this case a rogue wave of gargantuan dimensions swept onto the Norwegian coast and destroyed the entire apparatus. As of mid-1993, the decision of whether to continue or give up has not been made. It may be difficult to obtain funds for the continuing research. It may be that such once-in-a-century mishaps will have to be factored into construction costs and covered by adequate insurance, an item sometimes hard to obtain in the development and research fields.

Regardless of the outcome, the company did prove that the principle was sound. An invisible industry was made visible, and we took another step into the future.

→ *High-Tech Security*

Twelve-year-olds can eavesdrop on computers by picking up signals emitted by electron sweep beams crisscrossing video screens. Imagine the embarrassment of bank managers when kids knew as much about their largest loans as they did. Now a company in England, Pilkington Glass, has come up with an answer.

Most home and office windows are transparent to white, infrared, and ultraviolet light; to gamma rays; and to data signals. Political and industrial spies and terrorists using off-the-shelf "kiddy" equipment can intercept confidential data through such window panes. I've spoken to highly placed members of government in rooms that were public billboards to people who know how to read them. Governments are generally unaware that it's possible to detect such electronic signals miles from the source without physically penetrating any property, and that computer-radiated radio signals also reveal information to the initiated.

Pilkington's datastop glass blocks electromagnetic radiation (EMR) "broadcast" by both picture-tube displays and microcircuits. Such shielding is similar to that provided by a Faraday cage, a metal-enclosed room that protects people inside from outside EMR emission. Pilkington coats its glass with a metallic film via an electrochemical process that provides signal attenuation up to fifty-five decibels. The film, which reduces light entry by about 50 percent, appears as a tint. This tint also acts as thermal insulation to reduce glare and solar heating. Besides protecting corporate secrets, these windows reduce air-conditioning bills by keeping out half the heat that normally enters along with sunlight.

Datastop windows are double-glazed and protected against EMR emissions by conducting gaskets around an aluminum frame which is grounded to a metal screening tied into room walls. Computer operations don't have to be changed at all. Only building windows are changed. Secrets that previously leaked through the windows now bounce harmlessly around the room. Outside signals that previously entered the office now also bounce back outside before they enter.

And what about unauthorized people gaining access to a building? Many buildings, construction sites, research laboratories, and radio and television studios have superficial security checks. Usually these consist of a commissioner who has you sign a book and list the person you are going to see and then issues a lapel badge with a number on it. The idea is that you sign your real name and do have a legitimate purpose in entering the building.

You are supposed to turn your badge back in at the front desk, but you may not. To avoid this not-infrequent occurrence, a new type of time-limited self-destructing "smart" badge has been produced. It can be set for a four- or eight-hour life. Your name is put on the badge, and from the moment you receive it, the badge is silently (and chemically) ticking away. As you spend time inside the building, the badge gradually darkens. When your time is up, your name on the badge is obliterated.

The badge also has another feature. Suppose you sneak out with it, pass it to an accomplice who puts it on outside, and he walks back into the building. The badge reacts instantly to outside light and will turn dark in a few minutes. (This does not happen when you are inside the building, where the natural light passes through glass, thus filtering out the ultraviolet rays.) The price? About thirty cents each in small quantities. An even less expensive model, available for use in museums or by tour operators, costs only a few cents.

→ *Ferrofluids*

Almost everyone knows about solid-state technology, which greased the tracks for the high-speed growth of the computer and microchip industry. Now prepare for liquid-state technology, a new class of materials unknown in nature. Ferrofluids are a completely new type of material. They give us liquid magnetism.

Ferrofluids have unique properties. They contain microscopic magnetic particles, each about 6,200 times smaller than a human hair. When these particles are influenced by a magnetic field they defy gravity and can take the shape of their container, go upward, turn corners. Manipulation of the magnetic field directs the flow. A fluid in a dish can jump out toward a nearby magnet!

If an object heavier than the fluid itself is placed into a ferrofluid, instead of sinking to the bottom the object becomes buoyant and drifts toward the center of the container. There are considerable advantages to such a material. In South Africa one innovative company is using this "selective buoyancy" to pick out diamonds from beach sand.

Liquid magnetism is an answer just waiting for the right questions to be asked. As a sealant a ferrofluid appears to have no competitors. Just the thing to have around entrances during chemical or biological warfare attacks. In a solar heating system a ferrofluid could drive its own circulation. In medicine ferrofluids may be the new drug-delivery system. A ferrofluid carrying a site-specific drug could be guided to its location directly and held there by a magnetic field until its timed dispersal.

This could be more than a new discovery – it could be the start of a new industry.

→ *Nanotechnology*

Here's a real-life version of the old movie *Fantastic Voyage*: a "submarine" courses through the blood system correcting damage, removing debris, and generally surveying the human structure – from the inside – and reporting on unusual deviations from the norm. Tokyo University plans to develop a microscopic "submarine" designed for internal human travel. It could revolutionize medicine. Possibly such a mobile device could remain in the body more or less permanently. After all, the internal thermometer already has the capacity to remain in the body for a full year, constantly reporting thermal conditions.

Nanotechnology is the science of the inorganic invisible. (*Nano* is the prefix in the metric system for one-billionth; it refers to something extremely small.) K. Eric Drexler, author of *Engines of Creation: The Coming Era of Nanotechnology*, might be termed the inventor of this whole field. Nanotechnology is based on the manipulation of individual atoms or molecules to build structures to complex, atomic specifications. At the molecular level things act differently than they do when grouped together in the much larger clumps we see in everyday life.

This "submarine" is extremely small, not like the "bulky" silicon motor made recently by researchers at the University of California at Berkeley, which has the thickness of a human hair and can spin at only 500 rpm. Transistors were originally about one-third the width of a human hair. Today's transistors are one-hundredth the width of a human hair. At the Massachusetts Institute of Technology, experimental transistors are down to twenty-five nanometers, about 0.003 the width of a human hair – about one hundred atoms wide.

It's a new world when things get this small. For instance, researchers at AT&T found that a cluster of twelve silicon atoms reacts up to a thousand times faster than a cluster of thirteen atoms. The potential is monumental. Computers in a pencil may serve as translators and as robots that can see, talk, and react to your commands. Nanotechnology can probably be applied to both metal and ceramic materials, which could result in longer-lasting engine parts and higher efficiency power units.

A few years ago most scientists, including Drexler, thought it might be decades before nanotechnology made major advances. That time frame appears to be compressing. Advances in this field are accelerating much faster than believed possible in 1990. Positive effects of nanotechnological innovations in medicine and environmental restoration are now perceived as actually possible. For instance, the design of protein molecules has been followed by the design of a working enzyme unlike anything in nature. This could herald the concept of evolution-in-a-drum, methods for producing molecules that self-assemble to form larger structures.

The manipulation of individual atoms at IBM proves that precisely positioned atomic-level control can be accomplished. DNA has been fabricated into a cube. Designed and fabricated molecules are part of today's – not tomorrow's – technology.

As Drexler works toward building the first crude molecular assembler, Dr. Ralph Merkle, founder of Xerox PARC's Computational Nanotechnology Project, is working on proposed molecular devices, including bearings and other mechanical components. This is reminiscent (under a microscope) of Henry Ford's building his first car. With nanotechnology, the "submarine" could be built to cruise through arteries cleaning out plaque and cholesterol.

The Ministry of International Trade and Industry (MITI) in Japan lists nanotechnology as among the most critical developments for the twenty-first century. When the Japanese invest heavily, something is usually about to move. When Drexler first announced his theories in this field, North America's general response was, "Interesting, maybe we should look at this twenty-five years down the road." MITI looked at it and dedicated $185 million to develop nanotechnology during this decade. The journal *Nature* recently convened a conference in Japan on nanotechnology, in conjunction with the Science and Technology Agency, to focus on building molecular structures, materials, and machines. Drexler's book *Engines of Creation* has been translated, published, and distributed in Japan.

Media worldwide eventually noticed the growing interest, and such publications as the *New York Times, The Economist, Science,*

Time, Business Week, and *Popular Science* wrote about the possibilities in this emerging field. In Japan, Nippon Broadcasting Corporation (NHK) produced a three-hour television series exploring nanotechnology research and its implications for the future. In Britain there is now a professional journal called *Nanotechnology.* A recent conference in Monterey, California, featured ecotechnology with nanotechnology as a popular segment. Once again, tomorrow has arrived on our doorstop today.

→   *Electronic*
     Publishing

With a computer, everyone can learn to write, edit, print, and publish. Once people become publishers, they can serve as their own dispatch office, sending their electronic books to the world via fax, E-mail, laser printer, computer disk, and even CD-ROM. All this can be done at a cost that is magnitudes lower than the cost of producing the book you now hold in your hands. It is the intellectual equivalent of a front-end loader replacing the ditch-digger.

Power is leaving the hands of traditional publishers and empowering those with the right attitude – people with initiative, motivation, inquisitiveness, and determination. With direct costs of an electronic book limited to owning or renting a computer, a modem, and a fax, the cost of the final product is mainly those fifty-cent floppy disks. Naturally, time is important and valuable, but that is your contribution. After your book is put on a disk that is virtually indestructible (although it still pays to put one copy in a safe deposit box), it can be duplicated in as little as forty-two seconds, again and again and again. If you listen closely you might catch the sound of cash registers ringing. This is just what Bill Gates, president of Microsoft, did to make himself the richest man in North America. He's an electronic publisher who sells for hundreds of dollars per copy a product that costs very little to produce.

With electronic books, control of the end product resides with the writer. The computer that produces the manuscript can produce the finished product, right in your home office. The author now controls his or her own destiny. Authors who can publish the books they write have moved to another level. What is perhaps the biggest advantage over a printed book? Access to a market traditional publishers have never considered: that 40 percent of the population that can't read. (In North America about 20 percent of the people are totally illiterate and another 20 percent are functionally illiterate.) People who cannot read can still benefit from hearing your book. How? Electronic books can read themselves – in male, female, or robotic voice. People who cannot read have no trouble with the spoken word. Nor do those other billions of people around the planet who have never been exposed to vast amounts of knowledge because traditional publishers never gave them a thought.

A printed book like this one costs up-front money to develop and produce. A "manuscript" on hard drive, however, can be easily duplicated on inexpensive, almost indestructible disks. Make as many as you can sell. Notice I said "as many as you can sell," *not* "as many as you think you can sell." Make exactly what the market will buy. That's a luxury that the publishers of this book didn't have. They had to estimate sales and order a print run accordingly.

Set your price high. It will still be low compared to printed books. I sell my collected work as an electronic book, and my profit margin lies in the realm of the glorious, compared to what the publishers of this book can hope to realize. With my better margin I can do promotion, deals, and quantity pricing that is impossible in this Gutenberg format. Mailing in the United States, I can send my book – a ten-disk set – around America for under a dollar. In Canada it costs over eight dollars to send the same disks from Vancouver to Toronto. I can also manufacture the disks in Washington state at one-third of Vancouver's prices.

One joy of electronic self-publishing is that with little capital required to produce the books you can take a new approach to marketing. Consider your disks as samples, and give them to computer stores, to any wide-awake bookstore owner, or to the growing number of electronic publishers. The possibilities, because of dramatically low production and delivery costs, allow sampling on a scale no traditional publisher can afford. Imagine you have a new seed. Where is the fertile environment for it to grow? The disks are small enough and light enough to be mailed in ordinary envelopes or padded disk mailers. Mail disk copies to book reviewers. Be generous. At a direct cost of $1 plus postage, the first hundred copies are no big deal. To a traditional publisher, such marketing is costly.

Print a nice label. Present the dust jacket on the beginning of the disk. If the book sells, invest in better packaging. Good profit margins permit better packaging and better promotion. If the book clicks, go to direct mail order, where you get all the profit. Many buyers come from small towns that probably wouldn't hear of your book for years through traditional channels; or your buyers will be cutting-edge "teckies" who will buy anything they think will keep them riding the crest of the information wave. There are thousands of data banks, hundreds of computer networks, and millions of ardent fans lusting to soak up information by the gigabyte.

If successful, consider putting your book on the new flopticals. These floppy disks hold a massive twenty-one megabytes, from twenty to twenty-five times more data than the present standard floppy disk. My ten-volume electronic book, *Lessons from the Future,* is all on one floptical. That's in English. There are another ten volumes translated into Spanish and the floptical will shortly hold still more ten volumes in kanji script for Cantonese and Mandarin viewers.

If sales go well, consider a CD-ROM. This is similar to the 4.5-inch CD that rock stars make their millions on. To get a low cost per copy for CDs, you need to order several thousand. If you want to make just one, you can do that through a breakthrough in CD-ROM production that allows you to make a single disk for around $300.

(A new chain-outlet company called One-Off CD Shop is sprouting up throughout North America. This outfit made my gold CD-ROMs.)

We're now at the early stage of electronic publishing, and the late stage of traditional book publishing. An early edition of a Gutenberg Bible is worth $1 million today. Its value is as a collector's item. Increasingly, that will become the fate of printed books. They will be superceded, for economic reasons, by electronic books. And they'll become, like most of what you find in an antique store, relics of an earlier age.

The text of this book is set Adobe Garamond. This electronic version, designed by Robert Slimbach in 1989, is based on the original sixteenth century design by Claude Garamond, a Parisian punchcutter.

The headlines are set in Meta. Designed in 1991 by Erik Spiekermann, Meta was designed to be easily read both on computer monitors and recycled papers.

Designed by John Pylypczak, Concrete, Toronto
Typeset by Tony Gordon Limited

$30.00 OFF

If you are interested in taking the next step into the world of electronic publishing, this $30.00 certificate may be applied against the $150.00 purchase price of the complete 10-volume electronic book entitled **LESSONS FROM THE FUTURE**. The disks contain 500 chapters, or "items of change," dealing with the future, high technology, communications, and social change.

The disks are available for Macintosh or IBM/clone computers in either 3.5-inch or 5.25-inch size (the latter for IBM only). They are also available on the new floptical (21 MGB) disk (all 10 volumes on one disk) or on CD-ROM disk (also on one disk).

The complete 10-volume set of **LESSONS FROM THE FUTURE** may be ordered from:

21st Century Media
Communications Inc.
815 Harris Street
Suite #4
Bellingham, WA
USA 98225
Fax: 206-676-9435

OR FROM

Frank Ogden
548 Cardero Street
Vancouver, B.C.
Canada V6G 2W6
Fax: 604-681-0969

→ →

INCLUDE THIS PAGE WITH YOUR ORDER TO RECEIVE $30.00 OFF THE PURCHASE PRICE!